Perennial Wealth

A GUIDE FOR

Cultivating the Family Enterprise

A GUIDE FOR

Cultivating the Family Enterprise

Perennial Wealth

DANIEL R. LAGERBORG

with **TAYLOR KIRKPATRICK** *and* **JAY BRENNEMAN**

KAIROS

ISBN: 978-1-7336296-6-9

Published by Retelling, LLC | retelling.net

Design by Cynthia Young | youngdesign.biz

Illustrations by Yaakov Weinstein

For ADELINE, ELEANOR,
and the precious next generation in your lives

Contents

Perennial:
Continuing without interruption

Enduring

Persistent

Seventy percent of wealthy families lose their wealth by the second generation, and a stunning 90% by the third, according to the Williams Group wealth consultancy.*

I have seen time and time again that this is the key to multigenerational wealth: Not the wills and trusts that we set up, but rather our time, stories, lessons learned, values, and vision— our testimony.

*http://money.com/money/3925308/rich-families-lose-wealth/

Foreword

It can be said that great ones make the complicated simple. As one's wealth grows larger, all of life can become more complicated. Dan Lagerborg has conducted over 11,000 meetings with people of all levels of financial means. In *Perennial Wealth*, he dives deep into the family intricacies and challenges of the wealthy, helping them deal with the emotional side of being rich, the important application of EQ, the value of faith, issues around being a child of the wealthy, and the extraordinary value that a family wealth counselor can provide.

Through real life examples of family situations, we learn the keys to preserving multigenerational wealth, to understand what he calls Kairos moments, and how to hand down the family journey so that lessons learned might be carried on from generation to generation.

I have known, collaborated with, and even formed a sister company with Dan. He is what some would call "the real deal" as it relates to understanding and helping those families with extraordinary means. He is a dedicated husband, devoted father to two beautiful girls, and one of my closest confidantes. This book is a result of Dan's insatiable desire for those families with means to realize that they are not alone, and that there are ways to help navigate some of their unique and most difficult challenges. This is also a book for family wealth counselors, helping increase their awareness of these unique families and situations.

As you turn the last page of *Perennial Wealth*, may you feel as I did: enlightened, empowered, and understood.

Jeff Photiades
Wealth Management Advisor

Leading a family enterprise is a process, not a series of achieved ends.

Introduction

Do you know your father's father's first name? Or your great-grandmother's? I like to ask this question in client meetings, and in my experience only two or three percent of people know the answer. My hypothesis is that it's because they never walked the planet with that person, and that person's stories and lessons have not survived.

In a family enterprise, too often the tools and lessons that were utilized to accumulate wealth were lost when Grandpa passed away. His stories and lessons haven't survived and the next generations struggle. It's difficult to know where one is going if they don't know the path they are on.

Herein lies the challenge at the core of multigenerational wealth. If our *names* don't last in memories past our death, how can our lessons, ideals, and hard-earned wisdom survive to make a difference?

As a financial advisor, I have seen scenarios in which a family's wealth—both in finances and experience—has been bridled and implemented, sustaining a family through several generations. What these families have "done right" is what we've tried to capture in this book as best practices.

Unfortunately, I have also seen billions of dollars of wealth dwindle as it is passed from one generation to another. A Founder may have built an amazing structure, but hits a wall over someone to execute it. Often the cause is a breakdown in genuine communication between the generations of a family. But most often the Founder hasn't effectively communicated the Why: the values, motives, and lessons behind the wealth creation.

"Seventy percent of wealthy families lose their wealth by the second generation, and a stunning 90% by the third, according to the Williams Group wealth consultancy."[1] Countless families, companies, people's jobs, well-being, and charities have been devastated because of failed generational hand-offs. All these families had money. Money is not the answer. Relationships are the answer: relationships grounded in a common knowledge of the Why.

The purpose of this book is to give current family business leaders best practices to help them preserve the Why of the family enterprise, preparing for vibrant growth in succeeding generations. The most important step is to understand the Why and imbed it in vision, values, and mission. Then we examine best practices in communicating with next generations; identifying and utilizing the talents of family members, including the exercise of tough love where needed; creating an environment for growth; surmounting issues of loneliness; cultivating attitudes of curatorship of wealth versus entitlement; and capturing and celebrating the family story.

The experiences of many families have informed the journey that is this book, and particularly two wise co-authors. These two gentlemen have worked with many families who have struggled and crashed—or they have bloomed. We sat around a table in multiple sessions to dig out what we've seen as best practices that will equip a family for multigenerational legacy.

Jay Brenneman of Sage Quest is a psychologist and a family business advisor who has helped families with multigenerational business transfer for four decades. He has assisted many families nationwide navigate the complexity of the human side of family wealth transfer.

Taylor Kirkpatrick, president of Babson Farms, is a Gen 4 leader of a family business with incredible experience and results. He has navigated challenges with astounding clarity of vision and a profound study of best practices which yielded success.

As a wealth adviser and founder of the Kairos Group, I work with families to create a safe and sophisticated place in which they can provide for that which is most important to them, especially when faith and family are the most important things.

Perennial Wealth speaks primarily to the generation of a family enterprise who sees the opportunity to be seized now to keep the enterprise and relationships thriving. Sometimes this is the founding wealth generation. Jay Brenneman brings a deep understanding of the characteristics and needs of the Greatest and Baby Boomer generations.

Or it may be a Gen X leader grappling with how to move the family forward into a dynamic situation, besting the odds for family business survival. Often this involves healing the wounds from a family transfer of wealth that was not handled well. Taylor

---

1   http://money.com/money/3925308/rich-families-lose-wealth/

Kirkpatrick's voice and mine are representative of the Gen X crowd.

Taylor often reminds us in our sessions, "When you have seen one family business, you've seen one." All families are unique. That said, within these pages we have focused on the best practices that apply to all of us as families, that are perennial "bests."

The gardening theme is a throw-back to the normalizing experience of backyard gardening in my own life. At the end of a work day, or best on a weekend, I like to go out back with our daughters and see what's ready to pick. We choose some herbs to add flavor to what's for dinner.

Most years my family travels as if back in time to rural England in the summers. It has made a profound impact upon me to observe there that doing things correctly often has impact for tens and hundreds of years to come. In England a farmer showed me that if you pull the nails straight out of the wood, you can use the wood again. In the U.S. we rip up the wood and rebuild from scratch. A pile of small stones rest in this farmer's courtyard. When he has a little spare time, he cobbles some more stones together. In 30 years, he will have a cobblestone courtyard. In *Perennial Wealth* we want to cobble together structures that are resilient and lasting.

How do you get plants to grow, hardy and abundant, year after year? In our small garden, we've found through trial and error that planning is key. We've learned what crops grow best in our semi-arid, suburban soil: tomatoes, sweet peas, and eggplant—yes. Watermelon and cucumbers—no.

Preparing the soil is the hard, back-aching part. But providing tasty, nourishing, fresh food for the family is what it's about. And the satisfaction of gardening together.

Without over-working it, we're going to take you to best practices we've found to aerate the family enterprise, compost and fertilize the soil, and plant the right seeds at the right time. We'll talk about how to share the bounty and how to celebrate the harvest. We can't control the weather; we can't ordain healthy relationships or the events that augur prosperity. But we can work the family garden well, with best practices that have brought perennial results for many families. We'll begin with the Why.

We have written this book like a choose-your-own adventure. We recommend you read it front to back, but if you don't have that time or attention, visit a chapter as it speaks to a particular need.

We've provided resources to help you personalize each chapter, drawing some of your own applications. The exercises in this book and best practices can be difficult, but give them a try. You can lead your family in healthy change. **Leading a family**

enterprise is a process, not a series of achieved ends. We'll offer best practices that keep families moving forward. If you have questions in regard to applying these best practices to your own family, do not hesitate to reach out at www.KairosWest.com.

Disclaimer: Many of the examples in this book are heavily male. Please know that our intention is not to be prescriptive, but unfortunately it is descriptive of the landscape. It is currently the case that three-fourths of the wealth in the U.S. is held by Baby Boomers or older, and their leaders are predominantly males. The picture is shifting slowly but steadily.

A strong and intentional
testimony is always more
powerful than the most
robust estate plan.

1

The Tap Root: What Is the Why?

We want to lay aside the topic of wills and trusts, the legal and financial vehicles used to disburse assets. Most professionals disproportionately focus on the will, something for which they can charge an hourly fee. Instead we want to focus on the relationship side of a family enterprise as the crucial determinant of a family venture's growth and success.

We're used to hearing the terms "will and testament" linked. They were originally the same thing: one in the language of the Anglos and the other in the language of the Saxons. But we would like to divide them for the sake of clarity in *Perennial Wealth*.

We begin with testament, or rather what we will call testimony, and put our stake in this ground. Testimony is not an ancillary goal or a nice-to-have. **A strong and intentional testimony is always more powerful than the most robust estate plan**. We can't emphasize it too much.

By testimony we mean the Why. A will conveys *how* you want things administered, but if the *why*, the testimony, is not clear, the result is often contentious, and the continuity of the family enterprise is more likely to fail, or at the least not to thrive. To cultivate wealth that will make it past your death, and especially past your children's deaths, spending time on this testimony is incredibly important.

Your testimony is the Why that drives a life, that drove the Founder through wealth creation. It weaves together the fabric of your legacy. It includes some fundamental values and lessons to cast light toward thriving and abundant harvests for next generations. It is this from the Founder: *Learn from what I have learned and don't make needless mistakes. Here are lessons I've learned. This is what became important.*

Composing a testimony is harder than composing a will, because it's a process. As values are understood and adapted they are clarified. My friend Jeff says, "That which we focus upon expands." If you focus on building a testimony, your realization of its importance will expand. And the Why itself will expand in succeeding generations.

A great example of the importance of starting with the Why is Martin Luther King, Jr.'s famous speech in front of the Lincoln Memorial on August 28, 1963. Before cell phones, text messages, or emails, nearly 250,000 people converged at the correct place and time and heard what became considered the most significant American speech of the 20th century: "I have a dream…." King had a dream that America's laws would one day reflect God's laws. He didn't roll out a *plan* for human equality. He inspired his generation and those after with a *dream*. Because he spoke in terms of Why instead of Plan, people were able to personalize their plans based off of his Why: his testimony.

In Kairos Group, when we meet with new clients, we always start off with helping them identify the Why, the testimony; and from that the values, vision, and mission. From these we develop a succinct document of their goals and then an action plan for the next quarter, next six months, nine months. It could take a decade to realize the goals, because it's about the people-side of the family enterprise. It's a process. The plan aims to diligently and regularly adapt the culture of their family in line with the testimony.

The metaphor that inspired the formation of Kairos Group is the two Greek words for time. One is Chronos, the steady march of seconds, minutes, hours, and days. I think of Chronos as the march to efficiency: speeding things up, a low relative tax rate, a higher rate of return, a well-written irrevocable trust. These are all Chronos phenomena.

The other word is Kairos. These are the penultimate moments when time seems to stand still: the birth of a child, a marriage to your soul-mate, a near-death experience when your life flashes before your eyes, a victorious moment. Kairos moments are times when life comes together and all seems in equilibrium, all seems "right."

They can be simple moments. For example this moment, on what had been for me one of those tough days when you go your hardest and you end up further defeated than when you started. When I gave it my all, and yet today it was not enough.

I was sitting outside our small barn on our colorful hammock swing that we obtained in Guatemala (playing soccer with children from an education support center). I was just sitting, not ready to go inside yet. A bang and desperate cry erupted overhead in the barn roof. Tottenham the barn cat had noticed my presence and yearned for my company. I rescued him from the isolation of the barn and together Tottenham and

I sat there on the swing and chilled. It was exactly what I needed. Tots was a silent companion to commiserate with after a busy day.

Ellie, my seven-year-old, ran up, joy incarnate. She looked at my white custom dress shirt that was now thoroughly covered in black cat hair and said, "Sometimes it's better to make a memory and go change your shirt afterwards." She didn't say this as a declaration or exoneration, but rather a simple statement of wisdom.

This is Kairos to me. I cannot tell you exactly what my dry cleaner charges to clean a dress shirt or how many white dress shirts I have. I can tell you that Tottenham, Ellie, and I all found that time to be fulfilling. Actually, within five minutes I was surrounded by my family and we were having a lovely conversation over a fun fizzy drink my wife had whipped up, the perfect shift to a great evening. My life is blessed by my family who understand and live Kairos daily.

We can't create these moments or force them to happen. But we can provide fertile ground. And we can learn from them what matters most. What things are of value to us above all else? What are those matters of priority for which we will sacrifice? What are non-negotiables?

After more than 10,000 client meetings over the years, many of them for the purpose of transferring wealth and assets, I have learned that the focus on Chronos rather than Kairos is one of the biggest reasons why wealth and idea transfer within families tends to be ineffective.

My good friend Armen Khadiwala commented that paradise is not a destination. It is not a house in Maui or in Devon, England (my preference), but rather a state of rich living. Rich in relationships and interaction. Rich in what we call Kairos moments. The clearer you are on your values, vision, and mission, the more Kairos moments you will experience, and you'll be able to observe and identify these moments when they come.

Values, Vision, and Mission

The testimony becomes the basis, the bedrock, for values, vision, and mission. With clients we almost always work on values, vision, mission right away, because they directly inform and codify the Why.

Discussions of these concepts are morphing in current generations. Values and vision are taking the front seat. Mission seems to be the lingo of an older generation. The term "calling" resonates more than "mission." Or perhaps "purpose." But what we've seen emerging as a best practice is to break up the process so that values are identified by the family, working from the testimony. Then family roles in the business are identified, taking into consideration conative differences and aptitudes (see discussion in chapter three). Finally, these family members, armed with the values statement, work on the vision-making process. **There is one values statement; there is one vision statement; and then mission statements are developed for each of the family entities.**

Here's how it might look. Let's say you hold a jam session with your family and list values that are important to your family. From this list, have everyone pick the two values that are most important to them and share why. From this there will most likely emerge a theme or at minimum a discussion that shows the family values. Try to narrow these to two or at most three values. If there is a patriarch or matriarch present, coach them to wait several seconds before speaking, to listen. Ask a member from the next generation down to put the selected values into one or two sentences. Now the top generation gets a chance to amend the sentences. Pass them back and forth until there is consensus. This is your vision statement and descriptive of your Why.

Family values, built on the bedrock of testimony, need to be adhered to or the enterprise will fall apart. Every part of the vision statement endorses the values. Values and vision need to be agreed upon as a family and are then non-negotiable.

From here, the family may identify mission, or how they mobilize the family vision in their community in more than one way. Mission could be different for different family members and vehicles. Their mission may be described in one mission statement for their foundation, one for a donor advised fund, and one for how their family vision will be implemented in the marketplace. As long as mission statements don't contradict the values or vision, this is a dynamic and healthy approach.

Taylor Kirkpatrick describes a healthy family strategy as an armada and not an aircraft carrier piloted by one person. If that aircraft carrier does a Titanic, it's done. In an armada multiple people are piloting their ships in one direction in coordination with each other. You may have an aircraft carrier in your armada, but it's not the only ship. Everyone has their own ship, and the ship has a purpose.

Measure, Measure, Measure

Values, vision, and mission need to be driven into the warp and woof of the business. It's important to get them right, because people don't want to have to keep reworking them. Too many family businesses have cool mission statements that are meaningless in terms of how the business is actually functioning. It's important to create ones that are meaningful tools, and then keep them front and center without getting too prescriptive about "this is what you have to do." We have a great and effective example of this in the Constitution and Bill of Rights of the United States of America.

When the hard work of formulating values, vision, and mission is complete, too often people stop thinking. They stall out. They don't go the next step to work out the intended outcomes in terms of measurement. Nobody says, "The reason we're going through this exercise is that we want to ultimately have these five outcomes, and the way we're going to measure them is this, this, and this." **Measurements should be determined before implementation begins**: a matrix, for example, of how you're going to measure the success of your philanthropic efforts, such as,

Is every family member who wants to be involved able to be?

Did we use the rate of return of family funds as index?

Did we reach x groups in our community?

Measurement keeps the values, vision, and mission—and the golden thread of the testimony—guiding and relevant.

We believe that formation of this core is the first step to maximizing your legacy.

Testimony Empowers the Conversation

There are touchy areas in the formation of values, vision, and mission that must be treated carefully. One has to do with religion, which is significant in the DNA of many family enterprises. There are generational differences in language and outlook that need to be considered to allow for the fact that spirituality will be expressed differently in succeeding generations. Faith may be a key value, but a rigid track of how faith is to be expressed often does not work. It's not about *Are you going to church on Sunday?*.

The patriarch might say, "We should expand the Christian influence." The Gen X might say, "We need to act as Christ." And a Millennial might say, "We need to be a neighbor. Homosexuals are our neighbors." Now you've got a discussion on your hands! What is Christian influence? What is the place within it for love and community? What does it mean to "act as Christ?" What does it mean to be a neighbor? This is an example of how the Why must be maintained but interpreted and the *spirit* of the values considered in the language of succeeding generations.

Political ideology and lifestyle choices are other tricky places. When these are codified in a family business, there are likely to be negative consequences up and down the family line. **Guiding values should be a collaborative effort by multiple generations.** And, of course, collaboration is contingent upon communication.

Fertilizer

Test yourself: Do you know your great-grandfather's first name? On both sides of your family? How about your great-grandmothers' names? Ask this question at the dinner table or over lunch with friends. If you know a story about this person, share it. It is uncommon that we know anything about those who passed away before we were born. Teaching our children to learn from those who came before them is essential so that the hard-earned lessons are not relearned in every generation.

If you have not already done so, hold a family meeting to clarify your family values and vision.

If a family isn't investing in the social capital of the family, in building trust or communication or conflict resolution—the soft side—then even the best of intentions and the greatest planning for the future always has the potential of derailment.

2

Cultivating: Adding Generations to the Conversation

THE ABILITY TO PASS ON the legacy of family wealth comes down to the willingness of generations to listen to each other and to say what they really mean. That's not easy. Intergenerational communication pulls along a footlocker full of differences in what people have been taught to talk about—or not. So, the first step in communication is to be aware that generations will come at topics from different places. And each will think that his is a good or "right" place.

Grandfather, the Founder of the family business, might say, "Let me figure out the estate planning, and it will be fine. I've got 40 years of experience, and you guys are young pups and you may have an MBA from Duke, but I have ten Duke MBAs working for me every day and the way that these things have to be decided is on experience." That's a one-dimensional worldview that tries to reduce complexity into something less complicated. Not only is the Founder not equipped or used to talking about money, he has been taught that it is not proper to talk about it and that often it's a sign of weakness to do so.

In addition, he might come to a conversation not feeling listened to or respected. Maintaining dignity and respect for the Founder might not be achievable without knowledge of his testimony, including what he came from, what he did, and what those before him did to make what he did possible. This understanding gives perspective to his voice at the table and is important for next generations to have.

Gen 2 may dig in, saying, "My dad started the business. I've done it pretty much his way, and it ain't broke. Why are you messing with this? What's all this soft stuff about meaning and fulfillment and values?" Or, Gen 2 might be intimidated by or downright scared of Founding Dad. He himself may be near retirement age himself, with the Founder having hung on too long, and not be a real prospect for succession. These dynamics color his communication.

Gen 3 can represent a crucial pivot point for the family business, but may not feel that what he brings to the table is valued. Maybe Gen 3 is also Gen Millennial, and may say, "What do you mean it's not proper to talk about what your house is worth? Here, look…I'll show you on Zillow." Money is a topic that is not taboo to him. In fact, it's natural and it's important. So, when talk begins about what legacy looks like and what inheritance looks like, Millennials are chomping at the bit because they have been empowered with information. They are empowered with the philosophy of *if I don't know what I don't know, I can't plan. I need to know if there will be money there for me to pay for private education for my kids or to buy a house and when it's all going down.* Meanwhile, the older generation is thinking, *just let it ride because that's how we did it and sometimes there's some magic windfall and everybody does great.*

Younger generations can easily conclude that full-disclosure is the "right" way to operate, but the Founding Generation did the best they could, and the result wasn't too bad! Still, you can't say you want a legacy and also say *we're not going to talk about it*. **Generations of a family need to sit in a room and talk and listen to each other!**

Lots of the burden to achieve good communication falls to the middle guys: Gen X. They learned to type on a typewriter and a computer. They are equally comfortable writing a hand-written letter or a Tweet. This small sliver of folks is currently about 40 to mid-50s. They have also been called "The Oregon Trail Generation," the first generation to truly interact with computers. They can understand the oldest and the newest generations with their differences. These men and women can be a great asset in getting the communication flowing.

Hire a Family Counselor *and* a Coordinator

If a family isn't investing in the social capital of the family, in building trust or communication or conflict resolution—the soft side—then even the best of intentions and the greatest planning for the future always has the potential of derailment.

There needs to be a commitment to advisor-led family meetings that hammer out a code of conduct for the family employees, deepen conflict management skills, and develop a thorough understanding of Emotional Intelligence and how it applies to the current family and business challenges.

At a point of transition, considering the dynamics of intergenerational communication, **the best practice is to bring in a hired gun to ask the hard questions.** A family counselor guides family members away from conversation ruts and places of avoidance to productive decisions. A counselor ensures that people are truly heard. Without the counselor a participant might be sitting with the end game in sight, and how to get there, but he can't be "that guy" to bring it up, because the others will react to what he says, *Who do you think you are anyway?*

A family counselor can bring the infrastructure, the rules of engagement that will make constructive talk happen. He might say, "Look I don't know anything about anything business-wise, but I see that there are going to be these five conflicts that you all have to resolve before you can get anywhere." His job is to address emotional and psychological issues. He comes in when the point of the spear moving forward is a family dynamics issue that must be addressed so the family can get to the important things like discussing values, vision, and mission.

Here's a best practice regarding hiring a family counselor: **You don't just need the counselor, but a coordinator of the counselor**, because there will come a point when the counselor must be fired, must ask an unpopular question, or must be put on pause.

The life cycle of a family counselor looks like this: There is a honeymoon phase in which the counselor parts the Red Sea. But because she is hired to get to the deep, difficult issues, she will rankle someone and need to be fired.

If there is a coordinator sitting in the room listening and observing, the stopping and starting of the counseling process can be much less disruptive. The family may decide to hire a different counselor, at the coordinator's suggestion, and the coordinator can say, "Here's where we were before Audrey came. Here's what we learned. Here's

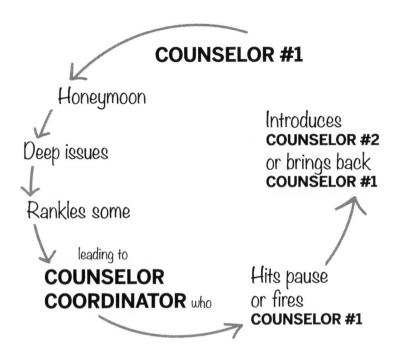

where we left off. Now, James, can you help us finish that and go forward?" Then the family doesn't need to start over.

Or, if things have gone well, the coordinator might say, "Okay, here's where we are. We've identified these eight issues and worked through them. Does anyone feel we haven't worked through them? Great. Audrey was fantastic. Let's give Audrey a break and bring her back when we identify the next round of issues."

The problem with counselors (although we advocate working with family counselors) is that to have longevity they have to sow seeds of discontent. They have to have something to work on. The coordinator who put Audrey on hold can see the wisdom of bringing her back at some point to continue from the base work. Without the coordinator, if Audrey is just terminated and James is hired, in order to find a need, James may come in and unwrap half of what Audrey accomplished.

Much of the work of a family counselor can be figuratively yanking the Founder through the knothole psychologically and emotionally. Often it is the Founder who initiates hiring the family counselor, to "fix the kids." Again, the coordinator is aware of the family dynamics in the room, although he is not a participant, and can bring wisdom of those dynamics to the hiring/pausing/firing/re-hiring process.

In the best case, Founders learn that they can develop EQ (Emotional Intelligence)—enough self-awareness to enter into meaningful conversations with next generations. This will push them in almost every case beyond their comfort zone, but EQ is paramount for a leader.

Who's in on the Values Conversation?

Let's look back at our discussion of values, vision, and mission. That crucial work needs to include key family members from different generations. Here is a sad tale: Two brothers, grandsons of the family business Founder, divided the assets of a family business into two companies, each taking ownership of one. Richard and his wife Jan worked hard, took seminars, employed counselors, to help them compose values, vision, and mission. About that time their three children, who had each been given 25% of the shares of Dad's company, all moved to a city nearby. They were following their own career pursuits, none of which had anything to do with Dad's business in the real estate industry.

Richard called them to the table, presented them with a carefully crafted (but not by them) values, vision, and mission, and expected them to work together, abandoning their own careers. He was forcing people who had never worked together, and didn't necessarily want to work together, and actually hadn't been all that close growing up, to work together in a non-merit-based scenario on the business side. *Because you're siblings you're going to have to work together.* Adding to what proved to be an impossible dynamic, Jan had assumed an active role in the business and, believing that one of the children was being treated as the favored one, tried to protect the other two.

This did not go well. Fortunately, the downturn of 2007 gave the father an excuse to say, "Time for you all to go do your own things, because this isn't going to happen for a few years." It gave him an out without having to fire them all, which he should have done earlier from a business perspective.

The time is approaching, after many years, for this family to begin to meet again. We will look later at some of the new dynamics that are making this possible, but needless to say they will need to re-examine the values, vision, and mission with both generations of family leadership involved in the process. A common language must be found.

Twin Big Conversations

For the sake of family members, twin big conversations need to happen. One is *How much is this enterprise worth?* The other is *What is its value to us as a family?* In other words, *Who are we in light of what we have, and how do we want to use what we have?* The two questions are matters of inheritance and of legacy.

Of the big two topics, legacy is more important than inheritance. It is of course tied to testimony and the values, vision, and mission. They are big turning-the-battleship questions: Everybody needs to cogitate on the testimony and values, vision, and mission to set a course. It takes time and often a family counselor to prompt effective conversation.

As to the inheritance conversation, *How much is this enterprise worth?,* **anything you can do to get ahead of the game is great, to prompt constructive communication before a catalytic event.** Even if family members are told what generally their inheritance is going to look like—it's going to be an even split, and it relates to these properties—then they have the general gist of it, and can learn and prepare. Very few of us are efficient when making decisions reactively. If a senior generation is not willing to have this conversation, maybe they or the beneficiaries are not ready to give/receive the wealth and different arrangements should be made. Maybe they need a counselor to help them.

Timing of Big Conversations

Often a pivotal life event cracks open the communication impasse: a health scare, a financial crisis, a marriage or divorce or remarriage, a liquidity event, a tragic accident, or a death. Sometimes the event doesn't directly involve your family. Your buddy's best friend drops dead on the golf course, and you think, "Oh my gosh, I haven't done anything for my family. I could drop dead tomorrow and we'd be in complete disarray." Some catalyst brings change and people know that things will never be the same again. The leader thinks *I've got a bunch of work to do, or I've got a bunch of values I want people to respect, and it's time to make them known.* Change is here, and the road ahead hides relational landmines.

The worst time to have the conversation about how much the business is worth is when there is a sudden death. "Full Kimono" meetings driven by urgency are not helpful. As soon as somebody dies, all hell breaks loose. People's emotions cause them to do weird and sometimes impertinent things. They have the weight of dealing with the tragedy, and in addition perhaps they confront an accompanying power grab and a money grab.

Worst case a family coerces one member (oldest sibling?) into the front to talk to Dad: "It's not me, but the sibs told me to tell you that they wanted to know how much money they're going to get when you die."

Best case your family has been thoughtful and strategic before that trigger event. You're clear on the testimony, on your values, vision, and mission to help chart a course when the road turns dark. You've had some helpful revelations of what the business is worth and what that means for individuals.

But perhaps you haven't, and the hardest thing about change is that in most cases it's thrust upon us unexpectedly. If you're not as prepared as you would hope, what do you do? Or not do?

An heir who was executor of his mother's estate told her, "The biggest gift you can give me—more than money, more than personal property—is a personal property memorandum." She did. Now he has a list in a binder that specifies *everything that's in this room goes to x, everything in that room except the two paintings goes to y*. Now he knows that his siblings aren't going to be critical of him when he's dividing up the estate.

Conversation Pitfalls

Two concepts that a family counselor will help you avoid in cross-generational conversation are polarity and non-dualistic (or non-black-and-white) thinking. Understanding these concepts and addressing them will help you get to processes and solutions that will be useful and flexible.

Polarity management sees or differentiates two sides of a truth and finds a solution to honor both sides. For example, say you're facing the painful reality that an employee, perhaps who is even a family member, is a 25-year stakeholder who has made major contributions to the business, but is no longer able to keep up with the technology and the demands of the job she was hired to do. The fact is that you cannot keep subsidizing her to the tune of $150,000, because she can't do the job. How are you going to let her go *and* honor the contribution she's made over the last twenty-five years? It is both true that she has been loyal and made significant contributions and that she cannot now do the job. It can't be easily addressed by a one-dimensional solution. How do you lead with truth and grace?

To start on the grace side of the polarity in this example might be a very generous severance agreement, public recognition of her long-term contribution, and perhaps, depending on her age and circumstance, a part-time position.

On the truth side of this polarity, in all probability her frustration with the new expectations are apparent in the department and are affecting morale. Leaders need to understand and sensitively address this. They also need to identify and act upon the best timing to address this change.

Dualistic thinking is basically black/white, either/or, and applying one-dimensional, simple solutions to complex matters. It will not allow for gray. On the other hand, non-dualist approaches always look for a both/and solution. It goes hand in hand with polarity management.

Non-dualistic thinking is critical when a couple of generations are circling about values involving diversity and lifestyles. Sooner or later a gay or lesbian member of the extended family will appear, or a difficult person with a personality disorder, and the answer is not *we'll quit being nice or quit communicating them.*

A non-dualist communication to a Gen 3 LGBTQ high capacity leader seeking employment in a traditional Christian business-owning family might look like this: "As you know, our family has long believed the highest form of human flourishing is in a marriage between a man and woman. And, we also believe God calls us to the highest standard of love and inclusion for every member of our family, regardless of their sexual orientation."

When People Need to Get Healthy

In the case of the three siblings coerced to do business with one another, an additional reason why hitting the pause button was timely was that two of the individuals involved were not healthy. One was haunted by addiction, and needed time to address his own needs and get clean and sober. The other person, the mother who was manipulating around a favorite, needed to gain the ability to exercise differentiated leadership. The work that the family needed to do on values, vision, and mission was not going to be productive unless everyone in the room was a healthy individual. If a person struggles with addiction, for example, that person is not going to be able to capably figure out the values, vision, and mission. **The meetings should be paused or an individual excluded if they are not healthy.** You need a group of healthy people who are all in the room and if somebody's not, the family should care for that person by allowing them to take care of themselves. The family needs to engage and discuss the person's health *and* how it aligns with their values.

Freedom to Do the New

Once a family talks and listens to one another, the ground is fertile for conversations that lead to taking on something new that they're not yet doing. One family business of apartment builders came to realize that they were still building apartments like they had fifty years ago. They trucked 2x4's out to the site, put a whole bunch of people out there, and built the apartments one stick at a time. Someone said, "What if we spec'd out our apartment buildings and then we manufactured them in one place? We could build according to spec, load them on a truck, and it would take three guys instead of thirty to build them." One of the sons said, "I'd like to do that. I'll take responsibility for that." Good communication fosters trust in others' ideas and abilities.

Prepping Kids for Conversations

Preparing Rising Generation children for conversations about the family enterprise requires parents to be proactive in teaching about money. **We recommend that you give children early experiences of making decisions about money in a safe environment.** Then process the experiences with them.

In one family foundation, every summer the kids are given an amount of money on the first day of summer. The age this begins is about 5th or 6th grade, but depends upon the child's maturity. The amount is the child's age times $100, so each year it grows in significance.

They're told, "You can do with this money what you see fit. You can run a lemonade stand, put it in the stock market, whatever. All we're asking is that you give back the amount you were given at the end of the summer. Anything you make on top of that is yours to do with as you please." The child who's conservative and nervous might put it under his mattress and that's okay. If a child takes a risk and loses the money, that's okay. But the money is still owed back, so they will need to figure out where to get it. They will learn from the experience and try something different the next year. Let kids try and fail—or succeed—in a safe environment.

This foundation encourages communication between these kids—siblings and cousins—about what they are doing with their summer seed money. They distribute a quarterly newsletter geared to the kids, with games like word searches for money terms. It includes photos and descriptions of the summer projects.

Another couple prepared their teenage daughters to learn about managing money by telling them that they needed to find summer jobs. Volunteer work was totally acceptable, but they couldn't sit around all summer and tan.

Later, when the daughters went away to college their parents helped them prepare budgets. They helped the girls center on what expenses they needed to manage. At the end of their sophomore year, the parents gave each girl in lump sum the rest

Age 10 or older

Kids' Summer Business Experience

- First day of summer given $100 x (their age) to use as they see fit

- Same amount due back on last day of summer

- Keep profit

- Share projects with extended family members via communications vehicle

of the money they would have available to get them until graduation, and they had to manage it. They both attended out-of-state private schools, so the sum was a bit of a shock to them. *Oh, I have to manage all this money!*

The parents worried that the girls might go overboard and spend it all, but the opposite happened. Both girls became spendthrifts. They were cautious with their money and chose to work part-time jobs while they attended college to be sure they didn't run out. The budget experience changed their whole perspective, and taught them to manage well.

Another lesson the parents were intentional about was to teach their daughters to work hard, but in healthy ways. Both parents were raised by parents who worked six-and-a-half days a week. This was not healthy, and they wanted their daughters to know the difference.

Finally, as the girls worked during the summers in the family business, their parents taught them that no matter what Granddad said about their roles as women, this was not 1930. The girls were strong enough to listen to Granddad's opinions, but also knew that they could do and achieve whatever they wanted—within or outside the business.

As you give kids the opportunity to save, invest, share—to do with money as they see fit—it provides a relevant opportunity to talk about money with them. This becomes a continuing conversation around the dinner table where you talk about concepts, starting really, really small, from the perspective that, "We're in a position where we've got to be more thoughtful than some folks because we're responsible for more money than some folks are." Eventually these Rising Gens will be ready to enter the big conversations.

Fertilizer

In conversations and experiments with your children regarding the use of money, employ the Scientific Method. It is a language from school in which they already explore. Help them to develop and test out the following around an experience with money:

1. The question
2. Theory
3. Experiment
4. Observations and analysis
5. Conclusion

Creating an environment in which next generation family members can establish their own mission, in alignment with the family vision, provides a fertile ground for leaders.

Planting Perennials: Getting the Right Human Architecture

MANY FINANCIAL JOURNALS believe a well-aligned family is more powerful than a public company shareholder group because their business decisions often consider decades rather than only quarter to quarter. Family businesses can win because they can look both short, for profitability, and long. Public businesses have to look from quarterly earnings report to quarterly report and never beyond.

Family business leaders know that somebody else is going to have to run this enterprise someday, and they are on the lookout for that person, for those people, among their own. What are family members' unique abilities, gifts, and callings? In a family enterprise you often have the freedom to create structures around these, especially after a couple of generations of wealth. These are all advantages of a multigenerational enterprise over the public sector. It is widely believed, and I have observed it to be true, that families who do this well, who are proactive in the search, can outperform their large corporate competitors.

It's imperative to get the right people in the right positions in a family enterprise, to get the human architecture right. When the architecture is right, the business will have its best chance of surviving vibrant and strong, with family members thriving in and satisfied with their roles. Family drama can be addressed in healthy ways.

Many families choose testing as a way to help identify individuals' strengths and interests. These results can give objective indicators of where people would serve best. There are many helpful personality or aptitude tests, but **we've found particularly good results—in fact we see a best practice emerging—for families who administer a conative test.**

Conation is action derived from instinct. The Kolbe Index tests how you do things best when you're allowed to do them your own way; when you're in what they call the "glide pattern."

In conative testing, people test out as either Quick Starters (innovators), Follow Thru-ers (Maintainers), Fact-Finders (Explainers), or Implementers (Restorers). These patterns represent positive characteristics for each individual. There is no good, better, best pattern. And they're valuable to know. For example, Quick Starters would be good people to initiate projects, but after initial phases they would best turn them over to Follow Thru-ers. If you've got 10 or 15 people, these traits are helpful to know, because everybody's going to thrive in a role natural to their MO (Modus Operandi). You can then identify what roles would be best suited to each family member.

It's like the Native American legend that teaches that corn, squash, and climbing beans make companionable crops, virtually growing together and supporting each other. The corn stands tall and provides shade for the squash and a pole for the beans. All of the crops thrive and benefit from the corn standing tallest, providing shade and support.

Once they know their conative characteristics, folks start to self-select and say, "I've always been philanthropic and am a Quick Starter. I'd like to lead the foundation into some dynamic areas of giving" or "I'm a Maintainer, and I'd be a good person to be in charge of policy and governance for the family office" or "I would be good at Implementing and protecting our values, vision, and mission." We have observed this knowledge to be incredibly valuable when a family member needs to step in and "fix" an ailing part of the business, because he or she knows whom to tap.

Perhaps a family member discovers her best fit is a role outside the family enterprise. Maybe the cousin who wants to be an attorney should be allowed to go off and be an attorney, knowing that she could provide valuable services to the business from her chosen profession.

I love the concept of the armada that we discussed earlier. The family wealth creator has constructed an impressive battleship. **Rather than looking for a Next Gen leader with the capacity to man the battleship, it's better to equip several family members, each moving within their skill set, as an armada surrounding the battleship and moving in the same direction.** Six, seven, eight of them can be empowered within their skill sets, and now you've distributed power from one person to eight. Think of the strength in that! The family may even decide to scrap Papa's battleship, knowing they are still strong.

If you empower family members to pursue and build within their own conative skills, in alignment with the family vision, you're much more likely to find a Rising Gen individual to lead the business. And if that person doesn't present himself or herself, you then can sell the business with good conscience because everybody has their own boats configured around you.

Identifying Leaders: Business and Family

One of the biggest challenges for multigenerational family enterprises is distinguishing between *family* and *business*. How does a wealthy family distinguish between being a family on one hand, and providing wealth and yield for shareholders on the other? All too often family businesses mix caring, loving, and embracing with the business of business. **Best practice is to separate family from business, and choose a leader for each.**

There needs to be a proficient *business leader* to run the business. And there needs to be a proficient *family leader* to look after the family, leading a family council. The aisle between the two must be maintained.

Family members should vote on a *business leader* whom they are confident will be aligned with the spirit and soul of the business. The family empowers the business leader to run the business, leaving the tactical business decisions to the business leader on "her side of the aisle." This might be an employee or a family member, but this individual's job is to run the business.

The *family leader,* on the other hand, regularly assesses whether the business is staying within the family's values, vision, and mission, and oversees the family council and family meetings. The family council provides education, like what it means to be a well-informed business shareholder. Let's say, for instance, that a family value is that all of our employees' children will attend elementary school. The recommendation is made to make sure all of the children could go to a private school. If the business leader reports to the family council, "You know what, we had a loss this quarter, and it's because I underestimated tuition cost for our employees' kids," then the family leader could either say, "We appreciate that you were in our value that everybody deserves an education, but we also have this value of good stewardship and you need to get profitable again." Or they could say, "Since it aligns with our values, we're okay with distributions being reduced because of it."

When the family leader crosses the aisle to make assessments on the business, a clear separation is maintained. The family leader doesn't meddle in business decisions;

rather, his responsibility is to ensure the family testimony remains intact, faithfully guiding the business. The business leader executes business.

It is preferable for these roles to be filled by two qualified individuals. However, in a few instances, families may elect to position one leader as both business and family leader. Even so, a clear distinction should be enforced between the family meeting and the business meeting.

Somebody is going to have to steer the battleship, or lead the armada. Who will that person be? If you find that amazing, unique person who is better equipped than any family members, they should be the leader. **But whenever there is a candidate within the family equally qualified to take the helm of the business, the tiebreaker should default to the family leader.**

Parents will often describe in retrospect some sort of early leadership ability that seemed to come naturally to a child. It may have appeared as early as the grade school playground. At the age of five, a youngest daughter rounded up all twenty of the dolls in the house from her two older sisters, sat them down on the fireplace hearth, and was teaching them how to read. She is now the general manager of a microbrewery and restaurant in downtown San Francisco. Not an easy job. Or leadership may appear on a sports teams or a debate team in middle school, high school, or college.

The skill that family business parents are well advised to look for in the next generation is organizational leadership. That is quite different from a high-capacity individual performer, or really smart child, which we all claim to see in our children and then assume it translates into business or company leadership. Not so much.

When the enterprise is yours, when it is composed of the people and values that you most care about in all the world—that's huge. This is a great benefit and blessing of the family business. Still, no matter who ends up the leader, the business should be run as a meritocracy, and the following traits are important to consider in searching for the Next Gen leaders.

Outside Leadership Experience

The Next Gen family business leader should first lead in another business or a non-profit. To have demonstrated leadership capacity is a big deal. This is so important that we believe it to be mandatory. Have they worked elsewhere through at least one promotion? Have they supervised or managed people effectively? Have they assumed leadership over a division? All this is good. It's for the benefit of the person to learn to be accountable in an arena that is not replete with relatives.

It will be easier for a chosen leader to build morale and social capital and leadership credibility if she's worked and developed these qualities somewhere else for even three years. Time elsewhere also gives a proving ground for discovering their talents and passions away from the pressure of family expectations. It gives some clarity to whether they *want* to join the family business, and in what capacity.

It doesn't have to be ten years and an extraordinarily successful career; three years seems to be a good minimum. Ten years might be too long and encourage that leader to plant roots elsewhere.

The collective wisdom of family business advisors from a variety of disciplines is that the one critical litmus test for successful next generation leaders is whether they have been successful elsewhere than in the family business for 3 to 5 years.

Start at the Bottom

The successful next leader doesn't often graduate in accounting and walk straight into the family business at 23. **But if they do go right into the business, there is upside if they start at an entry level job and at entry pay level.** It is important that children start in a place where they can move forward or up. Otherwise, if they start at the top they risk the perspective of sliding backwards their entire life. Personal growth occurs if he is exposed to the humility of having his family name not matter: "Who cares, Buddy? That's great. You've got to swab the decks just like anybody." It's a good slap-down for an attitude of entitlement.

A Gen 3 grand-daughter started as an intern in the family business at thirteen. Her supervisor asked her father what his daughter should earn in a wage.

"How much do we pay all the other interns?" Dad asked. "Whatever HR says about that, that's what I want her to be paid."

Grandpa was irate when he discovered that his granddaughter wasn't making nearly twice that amount, but Dad held firm.

Six years later the daughter said, "Dad, do you remember when Grandpa yelled at you for not paying me $20 an hour? You know what? I was really mad at you. I thought I should make that much because that's what Grandpa wanted me to make. But I just have to tell you thanks, because I learned more from being paid what everybody else was, and it was a great lesson for me, so thanks for doing that."

If three years is about a minimum time somewhere else, is there also a minimum number of years a family member should put into the family business before advancing to leadership? That's complicated. At least half of it depends upon how they interact with non-family employees. You also can't beat the cred that comes from experience, from being able to say, "I have my opinion, not because my name is Johannson, but because I actually swapped out that counter top, and I suggest we do more of the same."

But the bottom line is that he or she are not handed a leadership position that they didn't earn in spades either in the family business or elsewhere.

The Opportunity to Lose or Win

The family leader should have the opportunity to learn from losing as well as from winning, whether in the family business or in a previous position. Seventy percent of generational wealth fails because children are raised without the threat of failure, which makes it difficult to perceive it as it approaches. Failure is a potent teacher. It is inevitable to fail in business. The skill to be learned is to not make a habit of it. Not only does letting someone fail provide them with an invaluable lesson, it gives immeasurably more value to a win.

Purpose-Driven

The best Next Gen leader probably isn't someone who has awakened mid-career and decided that what they're doing just isn't fulfilling enough. Instead, this person is purpose-driven.

Some people seem to be born purpose-driven. They think sequentially; they plan; they put things together. Complex tasks and systems are inviting to them. They're systematic in their thinking. In the entrepreneurial world it really makes a difference if someone can naturally organize. This person has the unique ability to see the big picture and organize it. In the book *Traction* this person is called the Integrator. The next leader needs to be able to think four chess moves ahead and plan how to ultimately get there.

When relatives are empowered to pursue their own interests, it's easier to identify people with purpose because they are writing their own mission statement that aligns with the family vision statement, instead of someone else's mission statement.

Ability to Translate Vision

Business Founders are often individuals with unusually keen foresight. As entrepreneurs they have vision and extend considerable initiative and risk. They often had to work their heinies off to execute upon their vision. They may have been driven purely by fear of failing, or by the need to meet up to the expectations of a hard-driving immigrant father. The magnitude of their success may have taken them by surprise. One Founder surveyed a factory under construction and said in amazement, "Somebody's got to know what they're doing to have accomplished this, because I sure don't. I would have never thought I'd have something like this."

But Founders are often not good leaders. Good leaders empower others. This role is often for the next generation who are not as preoccupied with the demands of starting a business.

Warren Bennis, pioneer of the contemporary field of leadership studies, said that leadership is the capacity to translate vision into reality. The next leaders no longer need vision. The next leaders are not required to form a new vision. They know what kind of plant they are, what type of plant the company or family was seeded as: they're asparagus or grapes. Now they need to grow and bear fruit.

Gen 2 and Gen 3 leaders often fail because they're trying to replicate the Founder. **Rather, they should be using their time to understand the vision of the Founder and to utilize leadership to empower others to execute it.** This is an opportunity that a next leader should be able to embrace.

Lifelong Learner

Next-generation family leaders are committed to lifelong learning. They are on a personal transformational journey, including a journey to intentionally grow in emotional intelligence. They want to stay on the cusp of learning in their industry, and in the world as it is becoming.

The lifelong learner questions, she always wants to know why. When her doctor prescribes medication, she asks, "Why this? What will it do?" When an insurance policy is recommended to her, she says, "Tell me why." Many dollars are wasted by people who don't ask Why. If you don't ask others their why, your subsequent actions might not align with your Why.

Also, the lifelong learner sees and embraces reality. The business leader must be willing to grow into the world and to see the business as it is, not as she wants it to be. She must not only affect change but also embrace the transition.

Ego in Check

In the book *Lessons from the Top*, a think tank in the East identified the Top 50 best companies in America and then interviewed the leaders. One of the shared qualities was that their egos were in check. The leader didn't aspire to leadership or shove people out of the way to get what he wanted. He may or may not have been qualified for the job, but he was humble. In a family business that's super important.

As we'll discuss in a later chapter, it's lonely to be a generational leader. Ego further isolates the leader and the by-products can be infidelity, drug abuse, or other self-destructive behaviors. Family members, his tribe, don't see this leader as working in their best interest.

In contrast, the ego-in-check is impressive. In a University of Richmond leadership class, Generals Norman Schwarzkopf and Colin Powell were flown in on a black hawk to teach. General Schwarzkopf shared the example of how he would find a time in camp when the most people were out and about to go into the latrines, pull out the shit cans, and light them on fire. It was the duty of the lowest soldier. His point was *I'm the boss, but I'm not better than you.*

Expressed Interest

As well as being humble, is the candidate well-qualified for the job, and have they expressed interest? Do they want it? One of three sons came to the uncle who would be passing on leadership of the family business. The son had not aspired for this role as he gathered work experience, but on the other hand he had acquired, based upon his own interests, a specific skill set that seemed a good fit. He said to the uncle, "Ultimately we're talking about transactions and being good stewards with money and understanding the operations of a business. All that stuff seems to be in my wheelhouse."

"But do you really want to do it?" the uncle asked.

"I think I do," he replied.

In another family there were seven siblings in the Rising Generation who were treated equally in terms of being family, but not equally as far as involvement in the company. There was infighting and animosity. Some siblings were from a previous marriage and felt they weren't getting a fair shake.

One sibling emerged as the mediator of the group. He took the lead, and basically over time said, "I'm going to run the business, and each of you is going to have a component you're going to oversee, according to your skill set, and we're all going to meet as a strategic advisory board once a quarter. Everybody has to report on their part of the business and then ask questions of the others. That means that everybody is responsible for themselves and to each other. If a division isn't going well, that leader will get beat up over it. If the division is doing great, we will celebrate that success. But everyone will have a seat at the table and I'm going to run it." At the beginning people were skeptical, and there were complaints that one division wasn't as big as another. But given time, it worked. This family member had ability and vision and interest and took charge, bringing order where there had been infighting, without being ego-driven.

Tapped into Emotional Intelligence

It's difficult for second, third, and beyond generations to succeed without intuitive strength in emotional intelligence or intentionally building EQ bench-strength. Basically, EQ is being aware of your emotions and how they are impacting personal and professional relationships and performance. **Unlike IQ, EQ can be coached and developed, and the smart family will find a coach in EQ**. It is about the pursuit of bettering yourself, the pursuit of becoming the most level-headed, discerning, effective and creative leader or participant in your family business. Family enterprises neglect working to develop EQ at their peril. These are absolutely critical skills for the continuity or perpetuation of any kind of business, but definitely in the family enterprise.

Some healthy EQ is a great asset in settling ruffled feathers when the next family leader is chosen. Once a new leader gets the nod, latent family dynamics can take on a life of their own, particularly if there hasn't been good communication regarding values and vision. There may be surface consensus. *Yeah, he seems like the logical choice. That makes sense.* But underground brew dynamics like resentment and envy. People don't like to feel that they are not in control, whereas their brother or cousin or sister is, who might not have their best interest at heart. *Why should he get the spotlight? Remember how he treated me when we were kids? Remember how he always got his way?* Maybe they've always been competitive, and this is the final blow. Seeds of envy may be planted, and envy can be corrosive.

Additionally, siblings in second, third, and fourth generations often have angst over how successful they are, what contribution they are making in the family enterprise, and whether they are being compensated fairly.

Some healthy EQ and compelling vision can bring the needed elevation to conversations with family members who may be experiencing envy, greed, jealousy, or inferiority during a leadership transition.

Differentiated Leadership

Differentiated leadership is the ability to maintain relationships of significance while also being able to stay emotionally distant enough to run a business.

The family leader should have the ability and willingness to supersede familial resentments for the long-term good of the business. They shouldn't get bogged down in the nastier dynamics of human nature, but see the larger good for future generations as well as the current one. It can mean brain damage and heartache and enduring the slings and arrows of family members saying *you're a jerk or you didn't do this right or you are sacrilegious as to how it's been done in the past.* But they can lead with the hope, but not necessarily the expectation, that these folks will look back someday and recognize that they made the right decisions at the time, even if family members didn't recognize them.

If a mom believes all three of her daughters are equally smart, equally talented, and all three should be paid exactly the same amount of money, she is undifferentiated. However, if she's emotionally detached enough to say, "I've got three wonderful girls, each of whom is gifted and talented differently, therefore their roles in the enterprise are likely to be different," then she is able to differentiate.

Differentiated leadership is purpose-driven. It's larger than the emotional turmoil going on, like jealousy among siblings. It looks to the larger vision that would be for the best interest of the enterprise. And it looks to the larger vision that would be for the best interest of family members—even if decisions cause upsets at the moment. This is a requirement for next generation leadership.

In a family business it's just a matter of time until things get emotionally charged—philanthropy, business strategy, no matter what it is. A differentiated leader can recognize the emotional charge but not be ruled by the emotional context in which they're trying to make decisions or execute strategies. That's why differentiation is so critical in family businesses with its emotional connections and bonds and entanglements.

Transition

Transition is tough. When leadership is passed, the king is not the king anymore. Or the queen is not the queen. It's a seismic change that affects the person's identity,

Qualities of a Next Generation Leader

- Outside Leadership Experience

- Started at the Bottom

- Opportunities to Lose as well as Win

- Purpose-Driven

- Lifelong Learner

- Ego in Check

- Expressed Interest

- Tapped into Emotional Intelligence

- Differentiated Leadership

lifestyle, social interaction, and a sense of making a significant contribution.

Family members should be aware of how sensitive a time it is when the Founder or the patriarch or matriarch are on their way out of the business. The family has to help him know, *Hey, you're not the Furniture King of Kansas City anymore, but you're still a great guy. You're passing on legacy, and we're thankful for it.* And frankly, maybe he's become quite a crotchety guy. It can be a rocky ride for all.

Although many people are invigorated by change, nobody likes to be in transition. We all want to *become* faster, stronger, wealthier, or more beautiful. But not all of us are willing to embrace the transition to get there. We are not willing to consistently wake up early, eat healthy, work out, or be kind, which I believe makes you more beautiful.

But transition serves a purpose. It's a time of preparation to let go of ingrained perspectives and routines. In transition we pivot to look forward. But if the Founder has held on long, his prospect ahead may be unsettling or downright bleak.

Change without transition can create unhealthy addiction. For example, you could wake up every day at 3:45AM for four decades. Work hard and get home every night at 6PM. With all that work, some blessing and smarts you may become wealthy. Or you could go to Las Vegas, roll some dice and possibly become wealthy. This second version of wealth was created with no transition. That is why there are so many people addicted to gambling.

Transition can be messy and tough. No wonder it's so tempting to put off transition. Or to put off making a succession plan. You say you will make one, and you believe that you mean it, but you really don't mean it.

When a guy is 50 and his child is 12, he says, "I'm sure my kid will be ready to take over the business when he's 25." When the man is 60, he thinks his son will be ready at 35. When he's 70, his kid will be ready at 45. The corridor stays constant, because he really doesn't think his kid is ready to take it on. Or this is an excuse so the leader can shy away from the transition.

In one family business the succession plan was for the husband of the Founder's daughter to take over the chairman role. The husband worked in the business for 25 years, leaving his own successful business to do so, and for 12 of those years intentionally prepared to assume the chairmanship. He worked long hours including weekly travel.

But when the time came, the Founder couldn't give it up. His identity was so wrapped in his company that he couldn't give it up. He desperately wanted to. Actually, he wanted to want to. But he couldn't. The company is still successful. It has a great cash flow. But it is stunted, not growing with him still there. There is no vision.

This family brought in a counselor whom the Founder liked. The Founder did everything the counselor told him to do for about six weeks. Then he exploded. The Founder was holding in so much and trying to do what he couldn't do, and it just came apart.

When the Gen 2 husband realized that the Founder didn't want to grow the company, and that he himself didn't have any authority, and that it was a façade, he quit. His advice is, "I tell folks that you have to find your passion. Most people have it but are held back with some sort of stronghold, usually a parent. Take it somewhere that you can flourish with what you have." He jumped back into a business that he had developed before going to work for his father-in-law, and he also coaches young adults. He wishes that he had left two years earlier.

When you ask him what advice he would give to someone in the Founder's position, he says, "Communicate. Don't say what you think they want to hear, say what is."

A mantra we have within our firm is to "embrace the transition." I believe the Good Lord built us to require transitions to reset our wiring. But how does the family leader know when it's time to go? How will he know that his kids can really handle it, much less how long his mental and physical capacities will hold?

We recommend that when the clock seems to be at about ten years from what seems like the "now" point, that the leader go on a 3-week continuous vacation.

Transition

How did the company run while he was gone? If things went pretty smoothly, this may force him to start thinking about leaving earlier rather than later. Then, for each of the next nine years he should take that 3-week continuous vacation for a reality check.

Another good preparation for transition is for each employee, and especially the leaders in the company, to **create an operational procedures manual**, an annual calendar of tasks the leader does within the company. When does he pay taxes, do filings, bill out? These are annual tasks. Additional tabs can list daily/weekly/monthly tasks. With his first cup of coffee he does this…with his second cup he does this…. An out-sourced group can help with this project.

The operational procedures manual becomes a transition tool as well as an emergency binder. It may not be perfectly complete, but it's helpful to have a 30-page binder so that a successor can see what goes on. If a leader dies or leaves, a person can step into the job description that's been listed. Nobody wants to devote the time to this task, but it defangs the question of "What do we do now?" Roles and responsibilities are clearly spelled out.

Here is backwash that can attend a transition put off too long. The leader may be working with legacy people from relationships he's built who are not meeting the current needs of the business. As one of our clients assumed the presidents' role, he discovered that sixty percent of the workforce had been there five years or longer. He was assuming a loyalty culture. Unfortunately, the company was being fed bad information by contractors and had been for years. Employees and contractors had loyalties to the family, but they also had loyalties to one another in their small community and covered for each other.

The new president brought in a business coach to try to work with them, in deference to the loyalty, but found in the end that he should have just fired people immediately. In their business, with one-time projects, they needed a competent culture, not a loyalty culture.

Incentivizing

For a family to grow its wealth, opportunity has to swing open for rising generations. The Founder who built the wealth won-won-won. He got the spoils. But if Gen 3, Gen 4, or Gen 5 knocks it out of the park, they don't get the same rewards that Gen 1 did. They don't get the $5 million annual payday, because they are members of distribution. In one case that we've seen that the spouse of one of the beneficiaries has almost tripled the wealth of the family, but gets about $175,000 a year to run the company.

One way to incentivize is through carried interest, allowing someone to carry an interest and to participate alongside as a sidecar. Lots of times that works well if it's an outside and non-family member. He says, "Hey, I like my salary package, but I'd also like to take a 10 percent carry on this deal because I found it, negotiated it, and sourced it." It doesn't hurt the company if he succeeds. If the deal doesn't do well, he will feel some pain.

The key to in-family success is to change the mindset of family members and have them agree, in writing, at the beginning, that she ought to get paid market rate. Reality is that if she does not get a commensurate salary with perks and opportunities to invest like an outsider, she will be prone to resent the role, perhaps take advantage of the others because of this resentment, and create toxicity within the family. If an outsider would get it, and she is as capable (or more capable because she understands the institutional history, legacy, and family dynamics), it should be incidental that she grew up in the same house as another employee.

To not incentivize creates a malaise, especially among Gen Xers, who are starting to get bored. You've got to give opportunities for some big wins to keep the motivation of next generations.

When the Family Business Leader Is Not the One Expected

Moving out of generations where the leadership heir "had to be a boy," and where capable women were usually overlooked for a brother or her husband is inevitable, but a slow evolver.

A daughter-in-law joined a family after a successful career in another industry. The underperformers in the family got nervous. But the leadership choice came back to a matter of vision, where she was well qualified. **For vision to build something for several generations, a family must find the most qualified leader, regardless of sex or family position.** That person may be an in-law, and may be a woman, who is uniquely gifted to fill a particular role in the company.

In our example of the family business that was put on pause because of the ill health of a member, and also was waiting for the real estate market to rebound, the husband of one of the three children had meanwhile established a profitable real estate development company. Sensing that the market was turning, and that the time might be right, he approached his father-in-law with a proposal, a different business model, to get the company up and running again. Even the siblings could see that this was the right person at the right time to move the business to a meritocracy. The spouse brought experience, vision, and the EQ to relate well to the president/father-in-law by being straightforward with him, giving him the bad news always, but also the good.

If There Is No Family Leader

What if a family has enough self-awareness to realize there *is* no next family leader? What do they do then? If important conversations keep happening, siblings and even Founders can be honest when there is no successor. At that point, if some of the children are working in the family business and some of them aren't, the important question is if they want to own the company but not fill primary leadership roles. If so, they can bring in a CEO who is not a family member and be clear that the CEO is going to own a small chunk of it, but is never going to own the company. There are many such options if the family has become a circle of trust where they can talk about these things.

The family should be able to secure resources to find another good non-family leader if they want to. If they don't, they might need to sell. That's tough, particularly if the business is still delivering a product and serving a purpose. But it might be the hard, best option.

Tough Love: Family Members Who Should Not Be Employees

What if the business is doing well enough to support a family member who doesn't quite have what it takes to cut mustard? Should you support him? You might say, "Ah, let's pay him $50,000 and he can push papers for somebody." Is that actually empowering him, or making his contribution good, or is that creating entropy? Is that actually making him trust/corporate welfare dependent? **It's better to demonstrate tough love** and tell him he needs to find another job because the company does not have a suitable position for him.

Providing for Children

What about children who are not involved in the family business, but for whom you want to provide? How is the best way to give to them and maintain a sort of equity among siblings?

A son enjoyed his work outside the family business and was making some income, but not enough to enable his wife to stay home with their three young children, as was her wish. Dad, the family leader, thought his son needed $5,000 more a month to make their lives better. But if Dad was going to do this, then all of his children should receive $5,000 a month, and from Dad, and not out of the business.

Here's why: Another client's children all received pieces of their S Corps, each distributed in the same way by rule and law. One of the children is cocaine-dependent,

and the right thing to do would be to cut his distributions. But the dilemma was that to cut that son's, the father would have to cut everyone else's. If he hadn't run these distributions through the business, it would have been much cleaner. As it was, this kid was going to kill himself or the family was going to have to go for a year or two without distributions. **Best practice, take care of your children out of your income, not through the company.**

Combatting Family "Coasting"

One painful thing about family enterprise is that once it becomes successful, some folks stop taking responsibility for themselves and their destiny, two things that make life meaningful and significant. They can think, *well, it doesn't matter I guess, since I don't really have to work.*

The trick is to provide adult children the means to pursue their own interests and to create on their own, without enough money to destroy their incentive. Some wise billionaires like Warren Buffet say something like this, Look, I'm going to give the kids enough to set them up so that they're not going to ever be destitute, but all of the stuff that makes them think they're on the shoulders of giants, nope, that's going bye-bye and they've got to make their own way. I want them to go pursue something they are interested in. If they study polar bears, they'd better be the best polar bear studier in the whole world, because they have the opportunities afforded to them to do that. But don't think for a second that they can ride these coattails.

With a grasp on the conative strengths of family members, a process for transition, a good shot of EQ and differentiated leadership, and good communication, a family business can build human architecture to thrive and last.

Fertilizer

- Administer the Kolbe Corp test to family members. It's simple and inexpensive: http://bit.ly/2lmzxxa.
- Utilize EQ2.0 as a training process.

Reach out to Kairos for help with both of these resources, www.KairosWest.com. Resource: The seminal work on differentiated leadership is *A Failure of Nerve*, Edwin H. Friedman.

Selecting family professionals with a formalized process designed by multiple generations is a best practice.

4

Fertilizing: Cultivating an Environment for Healthy Growth

THERE ARE PRACTICES that cultivate a healthy environment for growth on both sides of the aisle in the family enterprise.

The Softer "Kairos" Side

Family relationships thrive in the midst of Kairos moments—those times when business meetings erupt out of control due to laughter at Uncle Joe's outrageous socks or when tender conversations surrounding little sister's breast cancer usurp reading the financial report. The business will still be there when these Kairos moments subside, but the family will suffer if you bully through and miss these priceless interactions. A beneficial side effect of protecting family relationships is often the protection of the family money. Relationships are the answer to perennial wealth for a family: relationships grounded in a common knowledge of the Why. Persistently investing in family relationships cultivates an environment for healthy growth, in both family and business.

The wife of a Gen 2 leader resented her husband's constant travel and the many people he was getting to meet. She decided to change her mind-set. If the business was going to be their life, she reasoned, why not pro-actively get on board? Not only did she start accompanying him on some of his trips to management meetings, but occasionally they took their children. This helped them teach their children about the business and about the stewardship of owning a company.

For Take Your Child to Work Day, these parents took their daughters to visit a company plant in California. "For me that was the best time of having a family business, because we all had the same business of being good stewards. And we saw it more as people than as business," said the wife. They saw their role as being stewards of the health and growth of a business.

The following key concepts feed to the Kairos side of the green and growing operation of family enterprise.

Transparency

Transparency in matters of family business implies both honesty and the desire to be forthcoming in sharing information. Transparency accelerates trust. Young adult members of a family, even if they're not involved in actually running the business, want to know what's going on.

We have found that often the older generation misunderstands the desire for transparency. Younger generations are okay not seeing information as long as they know *why* it has been withheld and *when* it might be appropriate to see it. They have an intellectual and also an emotional curiosity about it. They often do not associate ownership with that which lacks clarity. Lack of transparency in the older generations breeds distrust and a lack of investment in a younger one. Sure, reports could be complex, but with the help of hired professionals it can be laid out well.

A move toward transparency must overcome communication deficits from the past. Next Gen family members may carry pent-up resentment because of the previous lack of transparency. Nobody knows what was done. Nobody knows what they are part of. Nobody knows when things transitioned or how. Or, previous leaders may have used unnecessary complexity to shroud transparency. This may be because the Founder learned it the other way, that transparency breeds discord and conflict. But conflict is often the seed of a more dynamic family and company. Talking through conflict is an indication of trust. Trust is a fertilizer of multigenerational wealth.

A best practice is to develop a helpful, transparent form of regular communication. Find out what everyone in the family business really wants and needs to know. Ask them.

In one business, family members had distrust, discomfort, and a whole slew of questions about the business operation. The leadership made a major change to get people involved through developing newsletters and reports that explained operations and why they do what they do. As folks got comfortable with the process and the infrastructure, it led to more trust and better relationships. Family members on the periphery now knew what the business was doing and could figure out how decisions impacted them. Previously they would get a one-paragraph letter in April saying, "Last year we did pretty well." We know a leader who took the report from the year before, crossed out the year on it, wrote in the new year and sent it out. This was a $170M family enterprise run by a patriarch over 70.

This business now brings people in on votes for investment and similar decisions. It's not that the business requires their votes, but leaders appreciate that the buy-in that comes with being better informed is important. They want everybody to feel as though they have had some say in the decisions and had their questions answered. This is also an opportunity to sow more seeds in the family soil of values, vision, and mission.

The trustee relationship is another area that should be looped into good communication. Trustees should get to know the individuals in the family enterprise so that they can have an intimate understanding of what factors motivate why they do what they do. Often a corporate trustee has been chosen by somebody who is long gone, and they won't take the time or make the effort to learn what the beneficiaries are doing. This automatically creates distrust: *How can this guy act in my best interest if he doesn't even know me or spend any time with me? And if he doesn't know my goals, my hopes and dreams, how in the world can he make an educated decision on whether he should invest in something or whether I'm getting appropriate distributions?*

Transparency, if you're communicating the way you ought to, will create lots of questions. But there are answers to the questions, and answering the questions leads to good results.

Accountability

Here's the sneaky part about accountability: A leader who has introduced transparency might feel like decisions are now more visibly on his shoulders. Actually, he has dispersed the responsibility, the accountability. If family members understand important information, there's now an implicit component that says, *we have collectively made this decision, and now we're going to watch how it plays out.* If the result of a decision plays out swimmingly, high fives for everyone. If it does not play out well, hopefully it was a decision that isn't now causing blame on any individuals. Transparency creates a communal decision process: *What do we do now? Do we double down? Do we let this play out? Cut our losses and take the money and run?*

Let's say that a family leader thinks, *We're going to buy X and that's my decision and nobody needs to know.* If one day X is worth $18 and the next day it's worth $4, what happened to the other $14? If asked, he says, "I lost it." The blame is all on that guy. On the other hand, if everyone has been informed, and the family sees the investment as in family alignment, it's okay. Some people might have had misgivings or have pointed out that the business isn't appropriately mitigating the risks. But if they all agree and make the decision together, now it's much harder for anybody to point fingers. Shared accountability makes it hard to point fingers.

Accountability impersonalizes what is otherwise a personal performance in the way that it ought to be impersonalized. It's not a measure of a person's virtue if everybody had agreed upon the matrices of success.

The dynamics of a large family enterprise differ from those of a small one. You think a small group of four or five people ought to have it a lot easier. But it's a human system, and there are strong personalities, and these small, closely-held experiences frankly are more emotionally and structurally difficult to navigate than the big unit. The big unit generally has roles and responsibilities that are already spelled out, whereas the smaller units are more organic, which actually makes change more difficult.

You can get to an impasse in a big family or small: One person can be holding hostage the small family and saying, "I'm vehemently opposed to doing this." Or eleven people can be pulling in different directions in a large family.

Family communication facilitates accountability. When someone says, "I don't really want to vote on that at this time," it gives the opportunity for a leader, best case in a group that's face-to-face, to say, "I'd really like to hear what your reservations are." It behooves the leader to pursue the dissenting voice, to affirm that person, and to give credibility to the process. The dissenter then becomes less spooked about conflict or variance who may be thinking, *I don't really go along with this and I'd really like to tell everyone why without shame and without judgment.* These meetings also hedge against the occasional person who wants to say later, "I told you so!" even though they didn't. If someone wants to abstain from voting on a matter, push on it. "No, we need to all vote on this." Even if a person feels pushed to reply, you want that Yes so that if things get ugly he won't say, "I was a No."

Some people will drag their feet with a reply. But it's generally better to miss an opportunity because of one person dragging his feet than to go against that person's wishes without getting feedback and then have the venture go sideways.

A face-to-face meeting removes dissenter shenanigans that do not have legs in a healthy environment. Many of our clients try to have a face-to-face, and pay the expenses for it, a couple of times a year.

Accountability is a hard word. But if the family leader has the courage to create an environment of being accountable for your opinions, it enables the family to have healthy operational dynamics. Communication breeds healthy accountability.

Documentation

When opinions are shared and decisions are in, the results should be documented. Verbal conversation needs to become written. Meeting minutes, or a vote that occurred via email, or a follow-up via email confirming points of a conversation should be distributed to everyone involved. One family sends a summary of the last meeting before their next meeting as well as a SurveyMonkey poll on potential discussion topics.

Documentation is recording things. It's making sure that if we do have an agreement that everybody has a record of it by signing something or approving minutes. It's essential in case ten years later a participant doesn't remember the conversation accurately and says, "Oh, I would never do that."

Best practices digitize records and make sure that everybody has access to the same ones. Create a list of standards of what information everybody must have access to and be sure that they do. Transparency and accountability are a fool's errands without documentation.

Repository of Family Records

○ Contact information

○ Powers of Attorney

○ Passport numbers and expiration dates

○ Trusts and Trustees

○ List of professionals they utilize

○ Values, Vision, and Mission of the family enterprise and also from smaller family groups

Family Record Repository

The business can become the central repository to help family members keep their records up to snuff, for their convenience and also for the business when planning events and travel. A best practice is to focus on "Chronos" records such as powers of attorney and passports and to contact a family member when a passport expiration date is within a year out. This is a nice value-add for family members that also reduces emergencies and possible drama.

The practice to document may play to the skills of a family member who likes to synthesize conversations, create communication hand-to-hand with the family business leaders, and circulate it:

"This is what we talked about and decided to do." It's an example of something that can build family unity and communication. We found that many family members struggle to own failed ideas. A documented group decision creates clarity of direction.

The Harder "Chronos" Side

The business side of the enterprise is often outsourced to professionals who are focused on efficiency, yield, and time. Single family offices are evolving. For quite a while they were stand-alone entities that were so fiercely covetous and confidential that every staff member had to be an employee of the company and couldn't do anything else. They were secretive places.

Now they are becoming more professionalized, with a more open architecture. Employees don't need to know all the who's, what's, and how many's, but can say, "I know somebody who does that and she can help the family." Employees no longer must be family members as long as they understand the values, vision, and mission of the family. There's movement away from folks who are full-time employees toward either outsourced professionals or 1099 employees who can do bookkeeping, payroll taxes office administration, document coordination, or whatever the task as a fractional.

An interesting result is that when companies take on special projects, they can be more nimble. If they need to look at an individual aspect of their business, they can scale up that focus by hiring outsourced people, without pulling resources from current operations. As soon as the project is completed, these professionals are no longer paid.

Two Sets of Eyes

The challenge in adding outside contractors to the family business is that suddenly you can have nine professionals all sourcing through one person back to the family. This person can take a lot of arrows. They often find themselves at the mercy of two or three trusted professionals who do not agree as they vie for influence upon the family. In fact, the most qualified family member to lead the enterprise may look at all those arrow tips and remove themselves from that position because they believe they can't win. We have seen an epidemic of this in the last few years. How do you find the right professionals and get them in place without exhausting or scaring off the family leader?

The ideal would be to have two people, best case of different generations, taking on the lead arrows. If you can, get at least two family members who are responsible for a bevy of professionals, maintaining relationships with them. There's another set of eyes and ears in the room during strategic thinking, planning, and hiring. These two leaders determine how professionals will be selected, how to score and rate them, the protocol for how critical decisions will be made, and the time frame for making important decisions. Then it's not just one person saying, "You should trust our accountant because I do." The concept is a good one. Put two family leaders in place who have the freedom, with accountability, to choose resources rather than being responsible for mastering a myriad of trades, professions, and specialties.

All professionals must have the capability to work with multiple generations in the family business. When beneficiaries feel forced to utilize an advisor their parents' age, they often feel manipulated.

A Harvard Business School professor was talking about critical decision-making and compared two crises that President John F. Kennedy faced: The Bay of Pigs invasion and the Cuban Missile Crisis. The decision-making process was planned and intentional for the latter, because Kennedy realized how he had blown it on the Bay of Pigs.

Bobby Kennedy was set up to be the antagonist in the decision-making. They took the meetings out of the Pentagon. They had only two five-star generals in the room instead of four who wanted to prove their names. They figured out ahead the protocol by which the decision was going to be made. This level of learning and adaptation can become a strategic edge for a family business that a public corporation cannot usually possess.

Finding the Best Professionals

The two different-generation leaders should be methodical and dynamic in their search for the right professionals. First, they work up a request for proposal for each professional position to be hired, like an investment manager of a certain product or an administrative trustee, or an outsourced CIO. Then they meet with three to eight candidates and ask them to complete full RFPs, asking the drafted questions, including things like, "How does your fee structure work?" and "How did you react to your last failure as an advisor?"

Network to find the best people to interview. Meet as many folks as you can through conferences or family office groups, asking people who they use and how they use them. Of course, networking is a reciprocal concept. You have to be willing and able to give something to receive something and build a community. But networking can

Kairos vs. Chronos in the Family Enterprise

Kairos/Family Leader	Chronos/Business Leader(s)
• Family member	• Hired to shepherd a family asset
• Leads Family Council	• May or may not be a family member
• Guardian of the family relationships	• Ideally two leaders, from different generations
• Protector of Values, Vision, Mission	• Out-sources business tasks to competent professionals
• Liaison with family business leader(s)	• Facilitates the networking of professionals with one another
• Educates Family Council members	
• Provides transparent, regular communication	
• Arranges face-to-face meetings	

be a good investment of time and energy if you find the right people to bring the expertise to help your business grow. It is important to listen and filter as you receive referrals. Everyone likes to be validated by which advisor they chose, but do the key strengths of the advisor align with family values?

This spade work is good preparation to deal with potential discussions like this one: "Well, I have a new girlfriend. She runs a company. They are fantastic at this investment. Forget that she's my girlfriend. They're really good; they're the best in town. We need to invest with them." The reply becomes simply, "Great, but we need RFPs. We are scheduled to review our RFPs in August. These are the questions you need to ask and we will look at them." This also makes the hiring of the professional a group decision. If they truly are the best in town, the family member does not become the goat if it doesn't work out.

Selecting professionals by consortium rarely works. The best candidates will often get an allergic reaction out of one family member. **Having a well-planned process for selecting professionals, led by a couple of different generation family leaders, is best.** They *may have to make concessions on whether they like or dislike someone based on that person's alignment with company values or vision.*

If you hire the right sort of people, then these smart people can lay out for family members matters like estate planning and legal and accounting points of view. This accelerates trust in corporate decision-making. It's sad but true that we tend to trust the outside authority more than one of our own.

Let each family member get their own professional, on their own dime, if they wish. But these professionals need to coordinate back to the family-chosen ones. If they want to double-do everything on their own, that's fine—on their own dime. Don't fight it. But one master professional will coordinate the group plan.

Fertilizer

- Create a diagram of all of your family professionals. Next, go on LinkedIn and see if they know each other. If they don't, connect them. If you need help accomplishing this, reach out to www.KairosWest.com.
- Create a list of what information all family members must have access to, and how to ensure that they do.

Resource: Read *Freakonomics: A Rogue Economist Explores the Hidden Side of Everything* by Stephen D. Levitt and Stephen J. Dubner

The attitude of curatorship,
or stewardship, or being
philanthropic doesn't transfer
through osmosis. It requires
intentionality and mentorship.

5

Sharing the Bounty: Preparing a Mindset of Curatorship

WE CAN BE ANNOYED with what we see as entitlement in a next generation, but the fact is that entitlement germinates from a sense of ownership in the preceding one: *It's ours. We worked pretty hard for it.* In reality, of course, plenty of people were just as smart and worked just as hard as they did, but without the same gifts or opportunities. If we don't see our parents being generous and giving, we lack that paradigm and entitlement grabs hold.

The attitude of curatorship, or stewardship, or being philanthropic doesn't transfer through osmosis. It requires intentionality and mentorship. You receive. You curate. Then, as with precious artifacts, you pass on wisely and generously. The best way to instill an attitude of curatorship in our children is to model it in our own behavior. We model the thought pattern that says, *This was a great gift provided to us, and now it is my duty to give the gift to future generations.* What you don't want to say is, "We're in a position where we've got to be more thoughtful than some folks because there's insurance liability…And let's talk about some other things you've got to worry about… And there's a whole bunch of reasons why you don't ever want to get in trouble…."

Here is a cautionary tale: A woman who was a passionate patron of the arts and also passionately philanthropic donated significant pieces of art in her three favorite cities. She was laser-focused in her giving and she saw it as her calling.

When she passed away, she left her only child, a son, a $45 million foundation. Up until his mother's death, he had only ever given a couple of thousand dollars to a favorite camp. Suddenly he had to make distributions every year, and he didn't know what he didn't know. He allowed a handler to make decisions for him, because he was not connected to anything. He just knew that if he didn't give out five percent a year, he was in trouble.

And here's the conundrum: Surely the mother knew in her heart of hearts that her son didn't have what it took to manage $45 million, but she didn't intentionally prepare him for it. Now he's 50 years old and he's giving away money willy-nilly that was once used so wonderfully, that was curated well. It's tragic.

His son in turn is unlikely to be philanthropic, so that family legacy of giving will disintegrate. If the leading generation doesn't make use of teachable moments and important conversations, the rewards of curatorship can end quickly.

Teaching Kids to Give Their Time

Watching parents volunteer is powerful preparation for a mindset for children, helping to hand out lunch sacks in the civic park or help on a Thanksgiving food line or join outings with a youth whom the parent tutors.

Looking back on the experience of volunteering in his youth, a friend said,

"When I was volunteering, as most neophytes, I started thinking it was an act done for the benefit of others, but there were plenty of takeaways for me. One of the biggest things was humility. When volunteering, you come to realize that every person has a story, a story of who they are and how they came to be where they are. While it's important to remember that each person has their own unique narrative, it's just as important to respect, appreciate, and take the time to understand this narrative. Humanity and fate are often opposing forces and it is worth remembering that fortunate circumstances can change quickly and that every day is a gift. Volunteering brings with it a deep appreciation of all that you have in life, and helping those in need is a firm reminder of what really matters—like smiling, an attitude of gratitude, family, friends, and health. I saw my own life in a different light and realized that you never stop learning. I am grateful to have realized that developing new skills, discovering new passions, and gaining new insights were all possible through volunteering."

Help kids to find volunteer opportunities that match their interests and their need in order to expand their view of what everyday life is like outside their immediate neighborhood. Doesn't have to be elaborate. Activities as simple as helping an elderly person decorate their home for a holiday, taking them cookies, and hearing their stories can be rewarding for both sides. Consistency, returning often enough to build relationships, can be as significant for the impact on the child and those they serve.

Teaching Kids to Give Their Resources

Philanthropy can provide a door to larger conversations with kids about family wealth. It is a natural way to teach the importance that with good fortune comes great responsibility to give back to the community. **Rather than giving 10 Commandments of Philanthropy from the mountaintop, give kids the opportunity to work with it, to do it, to give.** It promotes the concept of giving while a child is young and still malleable.

Training Wheels Model

Get children involved in curating experiences from the inside. A family foundation was set up to specify that starting when a child reaches age 12, each year the child must make a philanthropic gift of his age times 100, so at 12 they gave $1,200. The idea is that the child researches and thinks about what they're going to give. The foundation stipulated that the intended recipient must be a nonprofit that qualified as a 501c (3) and must have an EIN number. Each child had to present to the family about what the non-profit did. Year by year the kids learned not to rubberstamp causes, not to get into pledges, and not to support huge organizations with their relatively small dollars. They learned that to have a meaningful impact usually meant to support a specific part of a program. The following year, the child was expected to present a

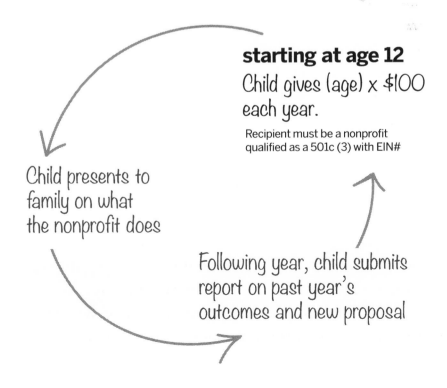

starting at age 12
Child gives (age) x $100 each year.

Recipient must be a nonprofit qualified as a 501c (3) with EIN#

Child presents to family on what the nonprofit does

Following year, child submits report on past year's outcomes and new proposal

report on the outcomes from last year's gift as well as the proposal for this year. This helped teach the kids to be strategic philanthropists rather than donors. Kids learned about philanthropy by getting personally involved.

This structure opens opportunities to talk as a family about the values of being gracious and giving back. From there, talk can morph to saving money, spending money, and the different ways people make money. How does all that stuff work, and what's a budget look like? If it's the child's money and a cause they believe in, they will be interested in these conversations.

Close to Home

Community involvement is a great reality-check for the child growing up in a family with means. When children are going to become responsible for large sums of money, it helps them to have experienced life on other sides of their community and see how their intentional giving can make a difference. Community giving and service is more impactful on children than sending a contribution to a cause far away.

A family took their school-age children with them to pass out backpacks with socks, hats, scarves, and gloves in the inner-city at the start of winter. They assembled the backpacks together and then handed them out. They found that talking with homeless people humanized them. **Giving back is a best practice, but giving some of yourself always has a better return than merely giving some of your wealth.** It cements that we are all humans, loved equally by God, just living in different circumstances.

Homeless people are lonely people; wealthy people can be lonely people. It is humbling to know that we can find some sense of connection together.

If you try to lecture a kid about giving, particularly a teenager, he may respond, "What are you talking about?" But if that same kid has $1,500 that he must give, you have his attention. He is experiencing his way into the deeper meaning and identity of what it means to be born into wealth and into a business-owning family. These kids are being brought into structures in a season of life when it's expected they will make some errors to learn from. But there will be satisfactions too. On a practical level, it's about service and about supporting the community in which they live and study.

Fostering Grown-Up Curatorship

At age 20, with $2,000 to give, a child in the same foundation with the Training Wheels model becomes a junior member and an outside observer of the board. At each age thereafter, they get a chance to carry more responsibility and more understanding of what curatorship means in the context of the family enterprise. They become a full director in this foundation when board members agree that they are taking their responsibility seriously, are making good suggestions about their own investments in the community, and are also asking good questions about other people's investments.

They have been personally involved in their chosen non-profit, and have not been giving to a charity because their friend liked it, but because it was something for which they had real passion.

By the time individuals move to the third level in this foundation, they are still stewards who need to be accountable. They get their ratable or allocable portions for what they're interested in giving. But they've worked through the construct to access the place where rules are a little looser. The lessons they've already learned within the smaller organizations are the same lessons that should adhere to the larger ones, such as requiring reports on measurable outcomes.

The foundation Level 3 creates a global giving report every year that shows what family members give to individually, if they want to submit it, and what they give to through the foundation. Family members see a pie chart. It's interesting to watch giving evolve. If somebody is big into ecology and sustainability, after a few years their giving might shift to early childhood education because their family has had a child. Or it might shift off of pets after the dog dies. Anecdotally you can see the trends of how philanthropy impacts people's lives and vice versa.

When the family initially created this foundation, there were disagreements until members established where the boundaries were soft and where they weren't. Was it okay to give to a college? No, because the school was not in the community in which they lived and worked. Was it okay to give to a buddy's fishing tournament to help cystic fibrosis? No, not unless they also had a real tie to cystic fibrosis.

Curatorship Across Generations

Different generations are likely to have different giving goals. The oldest generation is probably not thinking as broadly or in as integrated a fashion about training the next generation in philanthropy.

Rising Generations must be prompted to think beyond their own personal self-interests and their own emotional hang-ups: *Not enough of my projects are getting approved.*

Millennials might think that the way other family members have invested is not socially responsible. They may want to invest $100 in 50 ways to see what sticks, versus $5,000 in one place for impact.

A Giving Plan

Families with whom we've worked whose businesses and relationships were green and growing had two things in common in regard to philanthropy: They all had at least one arm focused on giving in the local community that they could observe and touch. It wasn't the 1040 Window or hunger in Africa. And second, they were focused on giving in relation to their values, vision, and mission, not their mandates. Be careful with mandates, such "It has to go to a Christian entity" versus focusing on value, "Our family values the way of Christ and gives in those ways." Let's say that a family values education. If they form a mandate that every gift has to expand the number of printed texts in the world, that foundation will lack relevance in a growingly eBook world. But a value on education might instead support funding libraries, inner city scholarships, and community writing programs. Each person in the family would be doing things differently through their own foundation, but they would all be promoting education.

Ironically the families who focused on mandates had one or two structures. The ones who focused on values had multiple structures, but these were like the armada vessels all heading in the same direction. It was fascinating to see. It was not one foundation that the family was hanging onto. The battleship, the primary money, was tied to involvement in the community. They all had multiples and they were all floating in the same direction. And there wasn't jealousy or infighting between the boats. They were value-focused instead of mandate-focused. If a family member wanted to fund a project in Africa, great. They funded their own ship with their own funds.

Family enterprises that seem to be withering tended to be more focused in giving abroad. But what they found is that if they weren't interacting charitably within their community, when their kids found something in the community that they related to, there weren't synergies between the generations.

So how do you integrate giving goals? Often a foundation is funding 32 favorite things, and there is no way to track them. The first thing you need to do, and it is a really hard thing to do, is to use your values and vision as a funnel and cut these by several. Be strategic. Determine the criteria that you will use. But with a focus on the business' values, vision, and mission, and with an emphasis on making an impact in the local community, the construct can be developed as a valuable tool. Thoughtfully building a construct reaps so many more rewards than a spray-and-pray get-it-done attitude.

Measurement

When you're excited about your giving plan, you want to be sure that your giving is making its intended impact. If it's not, you'll want to re-evaluate. **Along with your investment, request to see measurable outcomes.** "We're going to give you an amount that's meaningful to your organization, but it comes with these five measurable goals. We need a quarterly update and then an annual one. We will give you follow-ons if these things are tracking. If they're not tracking, we'd like to see why, what's happening out there." This puts the onus on the organization as opposed to on the giver to track down whether or not your dollars are making a difference. By setting it up in that thoughtful manner, you're getting a lot more data-driven information than most people do. Many organizations that could get follow-up investments don't because they don't have the time or inclination or ability to put together a report that shows specific measurable impacts. This provides an objective way to knock them out of contention.

Analyzing the overhead and expenses of organizations can be tricky. If the goal is, for example, to employ a nurse at every afterschool health care facility in the city, the organization's overhead will necessarily be high. This is different than an organization whose expenses are going to go up because they're going to host more galas to raise more money.

The parents of two daughters are raising them with the biblical concept that ten percent should be given away, starting when they first received allowances, at age eight or nine. The daughters could follow their hearts and choose their charities, but they were taught to learn about them first. They've been taught to look them up on Charity Navigator to see if they could say, "Okay, the money I'm giving is going to what I think it is, and it's being done in a frugal, efficient, and impactful way." They discuss their findings with their parents.

Most people like the idea of being able to give back to something that they care about passionately. It serves as a terrific way to make a difference in our community and to impart our values to our kids. It's an antidote for entitlement.

Fertilizer

Ask family members to list everywhere that they are substantively giving. Take the lists and divide the giving into three categories:

- Does it align with stated family values?
- Does it disagree with stated family values?
- Does it have no relevance to stated family values?

Discuss the lists. In theory the family should empower gifting in alignment with family values.

An unfortunate cultural characteristic of the wealthy and successful is to not talk about loneliness, fear, or anxiety.

6

Trellises:
Coping with Loneliness
and Burdens of Wealth

WHEN WESTERNERS VISIT a village in rural Guatemala or Rwanda, it seems to be a nearly universal experience that everybody they meet seems happy. They are smiling, unhurried, enjoying the day. Ironically, wealthy families who are visiting to "help" are often the opposite. They're burdened by worries and dissatisfied.

Why are wealthy people so often lonely and unhappy? How can we silo the stresses of wealth in order to engage those happy relationships and attitudes that we would call Kairos relationships? How can we cultivate more of those?

It's Lonely Up Here

A new client of ours, very successful, is in a master's group with six other successful business owners. Five of the seven are on anxiety medications. There's a lot of loneliness, fear, and anxiety among the wealthy and successful, and the culture of the wealthy does not talk about that.

Mark Twain said, "The conviction of the rich that the poor are happier is no more foolish than the conviction of the poor that the rich are." But when you're wealthy and a leader, it's as if you're not allowed to talk about loneliness and anxiety or expose it. Leaders of family businesses often experience loneliness without successful coping strategies. Consequently, there's a lot of addiction.

A unique kind of loneliness and isolation comes from extraordinary wealth, especially if it was received at a very early age. So what if I can drive my Bentley around town? It doesn't make me any less lonely. Maybe more so.

The Founding Generation are often most lonely, because they may lack the emotional intelligence to let them know that they're lonely. The older Founding Generations have a high level of independence and a low level of emotional recognition. They're less likely to know that their decisions are driven by angst and anxiety.

Loneliness can impact how they deal with succession. If your identity becomes so embedded in your role at work, and if work is where all your relationships are found, a fear of loneliness can postpone an appropriate timing for succession. You hear the quip, "Carolyn said she married me for life but not for lunch. She doesn't want me at home, and I literally don't know what I would do if I can't go to work." Transitioning leaders can be afraid they would be lonely, unmotivated, and have no purpose or direction in life at home.

On the other hand, if a leader tries to force succession and then realizes that the Rising Generation's values, vision, and mission don't line up with his, this too can make an older generation lonely, feeling more "on the shelf."

The Founder, the entrepreneur, is usually a workaholic, successful and aggressive. Often his son or daughter does not feel they measure up to Dad's success or expectations. This breeds loneliness in Gen 2, and they have difficulty loving or teaching the next generation well if they're still trying to prove themselves to the first.

Generally speaking, people 40 and under are more likely to say, "I'm afraid; I'm upset; I'm frustrated; I'm depressed; I'm angry at my brother because I don't like the way he's running things" than are their mothers, or particularly their fathers, who would be less articulate about what's happening.

But then the flip on what we see when you get to Gen 3 is that they have a low ability for independence, which can also create anxiety and loneliness. Gen 3 sees that Gen 1 and Gen 2 are not communicating with each other. Gen 3 misunderstands and believes this isolation by Gen 1 is one of their sources of strength, so they try to mimic the Founder and isolate themselves.

Gen 2 is often out of the picture. He is not going to start running things at age 60. He has not experienced a good baton passing. So now Gen 3 doesn't have a good baton passing. Poor communication is at fault all around.

Loneliness versus Solitude

There's a difference between loneliness and solitude. Solitude is choosing to give yourself space and time. It is creating margin and seeking a more contemplative rhythm of life in the face of constant demands on the business owner. Loneliness is

---

Characteristics of Loneliness by Generation

Founding Generation:
High level of independence; low level of emotional recognition

Gen 2:
May feel they didn't measure up to Dad's expectations

Gen 3:
May have low level of independence; misinterpret isolation
of Gen I as a source of strength

---

the inability to enjoy one's own company. The Founding Generation may spend their entire life building a business from high levels of independence and autonomy while achieving their goals, only to have their lives fade into loneliness.

This can happen for very powerful emotional and social reasons. One of the most common expressions from the Founder and owner is "this business has been my life." He or she is not accustomed to developing an identity outside the business. Even basic work/life balance disciplines like hobbies are too often absent in the life of the successful family business Founder. And the fact is, the business does need them less, often wants the Founder to "come into the building less," and the next generation leader actually needs them to create a meaningful next season of life on their own. This is a large and significant developmental task that falls squarely on the Founder's shoulders to handle for him or herself. The next generation shouldn't be strapped with this unwelcome job.

Stealth Wealth

The wealthy can have a hard time finding comfortable friendships. People who come from a family of wealth can feel a weird sense of shame because of the way people who are not wealthy act toward them. The ultra-high net worth folks seek out other ultra-high net worth folks as friends, or isolate themselves, to avoid this sense of being scapegoated or judged. They get tired of people asking them for things and being uncertain of their motives. And they get tired of the awkwardness of going out to dinner or on a trip and second-guessing whether the expectation is for them to pay because they've got money. Should you offer to pay? Should you offer to pay only yours? Then at the end it seems to go on your credit card anyway. Any problem that you experience people automatically dismiss: "Now that's the most First Worldish First World problem I've ever heard."

The wealthy may resort to Stealth Wealth to avoid feeling judged or envied or resented and to appear more "normal." When you want to avoid people's envy or anger, it's more acceptable to say, "I'm broke and my life is terrible" than it is to say, "Oh, gosh, I've got tons of money." You feel like you can connect with other folks better if you try and hide the fact that you have means.

People of wealth run into people all the time who have ulterior motives. Sadly, you can be good friends with a guy, and at some point that guy says, "We've been friends for 10 years. I'm really stretched this month, and if you could give me a $15,000 loan that would really help." Ten years of friendship is suddenly reduced to *Okay, now I see why we're friends.* Even though that might not be true, this is where your mind is conditioned to go. You give the loan, never expecting it to get paid back, and often times it's not. But if it's a small enough loan, you consider it to be an investment in their never asking you for anything again. You think, *Okay, I'll give you your $5 or $10 grand, and then I'll never see you again, because every time you come by you'll feel guilty. And you can't then ask me for $15k, because I'll be saying, "How'd that five go for you?"* The result is greater isolation.

Choking on the Silver Spoon

The sense of shame intensifies the more removed you are generatively from the wealth creator. If you are the wealth generator, your hard work and discipline are likely applauded. But if you're in Gen 3, Gen 4, Gen 5, it's easy for people to say that you're a trust fund baby, a spoiled brat, born with a silver spoon, born on third base. If you founded a business and sold it for $100 million, you're forever a rock star. If you received $100 million in inheritance and grew it to $1 billion, you were born with a silver spoon in your mouth.

You want to hide your silver spoon, because you don't want people to define you with it. You want whatever you're doing to be what defines you. You feel like you can never win no matter how good you are because you hold that silver spoon.

People can call you names behind your back who wouldn't think of using a racist word or an anti-Semitic word. But those rich wubbedywubs…. Like they think it's totally okay to use this language.

Shame is the right word for the feelings these actions cause. It's not guilt, because you didn't do anything wrong. But it's a shame that's a part of your identity; it's embedded in your name.

Special Shame for Spouses

Shame is compounded for spouses who married into family wealth. The shame can be deeper because they've not worked for it, and it can be harder for them to make friends.

If you've grown up with wealth, chances are your education put you into contact with people similarly blessed, and there's a natural convergence that helps you find "like" friends. If a spouse has married into wealth rather than growing up with it, finding friends can be tough without having experienced that natural social convergence through the early years of life.

If you're a spouse of family wealth, you may find yourself living with an intensity, of family relationships and family business, that are hard to manage day after day. A wife asked her husband when they got married, "Couldn't we just go away and live somewhere else?" If you ask her how she copes, she'll say, "I stay busy." She gets the laundry done, takes care of bank accounts, manages their three homes. She volunteers two days a week. But she says she doesn't have girlfriends with whom she can freely talk, except for wives in a peer advisory group.

Casualties of Privilege

It's hard to watch your kids struggle to find strong peer friendships. The hardest thing they have to learn is that when you grow up with more means than your friends have, at first it's really cool. Everybody likes you because you're the one who has all the extras. But you start to realize *Wait, are they friends with me* because *of this?* It's hard to watch your children go through this cycle and get hurt. Even well-rounded, emotionally healthy kids can be taken advantage of by their community and therefore be lonely. It's hard to watch!

Sometimes children make the mistake of using what their family has to elevate themselves and to draw people in. These kids may always seem to have a group around them, but they don't have good friends. When you utilize your wealth or your money to buy people, the relationships lack Kairos.

In one family the daughter, a college student, is generous-hearted, so she covers the rent of a roommate who can't afford to pay it. She tells her parents that she thinks she's going to get the money back. "Mom, I do have it and she doesn't," the daughter protests.

"Okay, that's really sweet that you're like that, but is that really friendship?" asks Mom. The daughter has gotten hurt many times along the way. Sometimes she helps plan events with her friends and everyone is "in" and she buys the tickets. But when she collects money for the tickets not everyone pays up.

When she began to date, this daughter was reluctant to bring her boyfriends to the house for their first date. She's learned to hold off as long as she could. She made sure that the relationship was pretty set before she brought her date to her home. When she heard, "Oh my gosh, I never realized you lived like this," it made her feel good to know she was liked for herself.

Kids from wealth can feel a unique loneliness from the pressure to measure up to a family name. A friend attended a prep school in a class where ten kids were from families that were household names. Of the ten, five are now incredibly wonderful contributing members of society doing things that are interesting and fun. The other five have either completely fallen off the radar or have died or they committed suicide because the pressure of the name was too much, or the expectation that they were falling short was too much. This is despite the fact that everybody at that school was talented. There were no free rides.

A phrase bandied around is *casualties of privilege*. It represents those kids who would do cocaine lines off their dad's face pictured on the cover of *Fortune* because Dad didn't seem to love them, but he sent them to school with a big wad of cash and said, "We'll see you when you go to Harvard." People wonder how a kid like this went off the rails so badly, when he had been given every opportunity. But of course, it makes perfect sense if he didn't feel he was paid attention to or appreciated or understood by his parents. He was inconvenient, yet he had to measure up to a family standard. You can see how acting out probably garnered him attention. Perhaps his parents were lonely themselves, and not in a condition to identify the pain and loneliness of their son. Wealth is a sharp double-edged sword.

Peer Advisory Groups

Where do you find relationships to buffer the loneliness? One alternative is CEO peer advisory groups. These groups are growing as more and more of the generation of C-suite people choose them.

Groups like Vistage or Convene or YPO foster camaraderie on shared adventures such as camping or rafting trips. Everybody feels like they've been through an experience together. Afterward they have bonding moments when everyone can talk in a judgment-free zone with people whom they would consider to be contemporaries. They don't have to worry about people ripping them off. People don't care whether you paid for the dinner. So, it can be a comfortable group.

The spirit of these groups is to talk about business enterprises and it is not always appropriate to talk about loneliness or worries of the heart. It's not what these groups are for.

But the issue of trust is a natural concern in peer advisory groups. Everybody wants to talk about their loneliness, but they fear they might disclose something that is going to impinge upon a relationship. *Is something I'm sharing going to be a breach of confidentiality? Will this information be used against me? Is someone going to feel they now have leverage on me, and can take advantage of me?*

Most of these groups don't get all the way down to loneliness and discouragement and anxiety. But many members of these groups admit it's enormously helpful for addressing the issue of isolation. Because success and wealth often lead to isolation. A group of people you can empathize with and they with you is of great value.

Mentors

Peer groups can be great, but what about the vacuum of leadership sitting underneath them? Is the Greatest Generation sitting at their country clubs playing cards with their peers but not able to be vulnerable and invest in somebody in the generation below them? The golden ring is to grab someone in the generation below you and also someone in the generation above you with whom to fraternize.

We've recommended that clients find a mentor or mentee. One G2 leader is in relationship with a leader in the generation above him, and he finds it stretching and stimulating. He feels the subtle pressure to demonstrate that he has the chops to make an interesting two-way conversation. When the wealth creator friend asks him, "What are you looking at and how are you seeing the world, and what is your perspective on this?" it requires thoughtful answers from him. He feels that if he's just a passive recipient of a mentor's information, the elder may tire of the relationship quickly. It's beneficial to both of them for him to rise to his mentor's level collegially and mentally, bringing a very different set of experiences and skills.

In mentor/mentee relationships, whether you're in the up-generation or down-generation, it's best practice to first articulate both of your expectations from the relationship. It may be fun to sit around and pontificate, but that doesn't move the ball forward, and the time together will not be priority for either of you. It's key that a person is challenging your perspective. The younger is saying, "I think it's interesting that you did it that way. Let me tell you how the world has changed since you made those decisions. Here's the new paradigm." The older says, "Have you thought about how this decision impacted these three people whom you might not be thinking about? When I made this decision, I learned…."

A Founder who is still going into the office regularly is putting the time to good advantage if they are intentionally mentoring.

Faith-based Communities

Many families of wealth pay attention to their faith roots in Jewish, Muslim, or Christian traditions. There are over-arching tenets, such as the belief that we're here for a reason and "you can't take it with you" that create a seedbed to think more in terms of purpose, calling, values, and vision.

Faith brings help for worry. Worry is believing you're responsible for something not under your control. A lot of worry comes from believing that you're carrying X people on your shoulders, whether it's your family, your company, your employees, or your siblings. You just keep throwing people onto your shoulders. Anxiety rears its head and you may eventually snap. A person of faith senses that Somebody Else is running alongside them and carrying that weight, so that it's not so crushing.

A faith community can be—not always, but more than most other social architectures—equalizing in the sense that people aren't as concerned about, and don't naturally isolate, people of wealth. This dilutes a sense of isolation.

Your Spouse

If you're lucky enough to have a spouse whom you consider your partner and best friend, this can be a great relief valve for loneliness and isolation. The challenge is that in a family business if you're griping about a situation in the business, and it involves family members, your spouse may take the situation too personally on your behalf. If you share things in confidence with your spouse, will she be fuming at the next Thanksgiving dinner? It requires great differentiation to be a spouse who is a sounding board. Still, this is a better situation than the attitude that is still prevalent in top generations of "I keep the missus out of the business."

Many spouses who are close confidants don't understand much about the workings of the business from the operational side. But this doesn't mean they can't be helpful in matters of human nature, in seeing the ways in which the family is working together—or not. **Your spouse often understands the important Kairos aspects of the family enterprise better than anyone else you could use as a sounding board.**

Buddies

In the cave of isolation, there's nothing quite like a buddy, an honest, trusted friend. Often it's someone who has no relationship whatsoever to your family enterprise. It might be a college roommate, someone you served with in the military, or a friend from a job years ago. But this buddy must be able to call you out unsolicited. And that trait should be reciprocal. Strong friendships can withstand that.

These tough friendships are built and enjoyed at a hunting camp or on a ski trip or building houses for Habitat—someplace where you spend a concentrated amount of time away from your homes with shared experiences and surroundings that lend themselves to having some of those deep, unhurried conversations. It's what the peer advisory group model strives for, but on a more personal one-to-one level.

If you haven't formed these relationships outside of work, you need to figure out what you're passionate about—or could be passionate about—and immerse yourself into it deeply with one person or a small group of people. It's not just a casual "we get together once a week/month/year for a few hours and play golf." It could be volunteer work at a museum or teaching at a local college or fly-tying or serving on an HOA board. Embed yourself in some situation where you will create those friendships by hook or by crook. Do something together that you both/all enjoy and that necessitates extended times together.

While there may be little you can do to educate friends on the burdens of the wealthy or to disarm their judgment, you can be intentional about cultivating supportive relationships with peers and family. You don't need to carry the burden of wealth in loneliness or shame. Cultivating perennial wealth is nothing to be ashamed of.

Relationships that Buffer Loneliness

RELATIONSHIP	BENEFITS	DRAW-BACKS
Peer Advisory Groups	Comfortable group of wealthy	Concern over breach of confidentiality
Mentors	Shared perspectives	Can lose priority unless shared expectations
Faith-based Communities	Alleviates worry; socially equalizing	Human desires sometimes confused with God's will
Spouse	Understanding of family dynamics	May take family disagreements too personally
Buddies	Call out as necessary	Require mutual interests and investment of time

Fertilizer

If loneliness, worry, or anxiety are dominant in your experience, engage in EQ2.0 training. Contact www.KairosWest.com for a trained counselor.

If you believe in God, spend time with Him daily. Spend equal amounts of time in prayer and meditation on each phrase of the Lord's Prayer. Whether you are a Christian or not, the Lord's Prayer rotates you through different themes that can help you realize your proper place in the greater world, often decreasing worry. While this is from the Bible, it is an exercise valuable for anyone who believes in a higher power. (Matthew 6: 9-13)

Storytelling can help smooth leadership transition by memorializing the retiring generation and opening a new chapter for the rising leader.

7

Harvest Stories: Celebrations Big and Small

THE THRIVING FAMILY enterprise celebrates its people well, for several reasons. It has the distinct privilege of celebrating both Chronos moments of achieving goals and Kairos moments of meeting personal milestones. Often the sphere of both Chronos and Kairos celebrations extends past family to key employees who see themselves as kin. Everyone, family member or not, gathers under the family umbrella. Employees give and expect loyalty. They matter. Celebrations of different sizes can serve different purposes.

Celebrate Small

It's a great morale boost if you find those moments that have nothing to do with wealth, nothing to do with anything other than to celebrate a person or the group collectively, and honor them.

Every morning at 9:30AM the 50 employees of one family enterprise take a breakfast break. They know what to count on each day of the week. Monday they're served donuts. Tuesday it's breakfast sandwiches from Chick-Fil-A. Wednesday is bagels. Thursday they get biscuits and gravy *and* the CEO brings in chocolate chip cookies that he has baked. On Friday it's back to pastries.

Once a month they gather for lunch and the CEO gives a brief State of the Union and recognizes those with a work anniversary that month. The staff feels cared for and these events meld the "back office" and the "front office" employees, family members and not family. And they are reminders and anchors of the business values.

Celebrating success, abundance, and remarkable talent is important. It's easy to get caught up in the grind rather than to take a step back and recognize the good fortunes that have led to this moment in time. A milestone birthday or anniversary, a new baby, or a special honor might not be work-stopping events, but are causes for some type of recognition. As you celebrate an individual's story you incorporate their Kairos into the larger family story.

Celebrate Family

Families used to live close to each other, and you'd hear the same family stories umpteen times. Junior would build a house on a neighboring lot, and multigenerations gathered on summer evenings for impromptu backyard picnics or to sit on the front porch. Before long someone would be repeating one of the family favorites and everyone would burst out laughing.

Today an extended family lives in different states, often in different countries, and the likelihood that you're going to get everyone together to share that experience is low, but worth the effort to try.

A family gathering might seem easy to put off while the top generation is in good health. But that moment can slip away quickly. And besides, how about doing it while they can fully enjoy it too?

Sadly, people in a financial position to create opportunities for family gatherings can get wrapped around the axle on the logistics and the dollars. Thirty grand today isn't going to have a meaningful impact on your life in the long run. But if it means you're able to gather all these people together to create cohesion and to celebrate the family testimony, it would be a tragedy to let pass by. The planning might seem daunting, but often there is a family member who would coordinate it. If you don't do it, it may never happen, and the loss would be great. We can't think of a single example where a client has invested in a family gathering and not found it a good return in the long run.

Each generation has a reason to gather and discuss the family testimony. For the senior generation it can be about education. For the younger generation it can be about comprehension. It's important to have fertile soil for all generations when the family gets together. **The best practice is that somebody with passion for the event plans it well so that people want to come**. When that ends up costing money and travel, expense, don't sweat it.

Planning well means there will be a couple of hours of Chronos meeting interspersed in mostly fun Kairos-building activities. Maybe you'll go over the annual report and ask questions for two or three hours over the course of four days. In between you may tour the family homestead, take a boat ride, visit the family cemetery, and enjoy a family picnic with relays and multigeneration games. Each of the kids can plant a tree on the family property. Make it rich with shared stories: "You're not going to believe this, but we were playing tennis right here, and your dad got hit in the face with the ball, and it was the funniest thing I ever saw." "I remember when I was a kid I shook up a Coke can and when I opened it, it sprayed all over Grandma."

Often family gatherings commemorate something like a milestone birthday for Grandpa or the anniversary of Mom and Dad's marriage. These are good "excuses" to gather the family.

Considerations in Planning a Family Gathering

○ Make this gathering a priority; don't wait or over-complicate it

○ Find a capable family member to plan it

○ Balance a few hours of business (Chronos) with several hours of fun (Kairos)

○ Commemorate a family milestone or remembrance

○ Choose a location to align with values, vision, mission

○ Add to shared family stories, including the Founder's Testimony

Occasionally the purpose of a family gathering is to ritualize and process a difficult collective memory. A family business counselor sat in a meeting where a family member mentioned out of the blue, "It's two weeks until the 10th Anniversary."

"Tenth anniversary of what? What's this about?" the counselor asked.

He discovered that it was about the death of Gen 3 Bobby from cancer at 10-years-old. "We never talk about Bobby," a family member explained. The family had not been able to integrate Bobby into the narrative of the family. It was just too painful.

With the counselor's help this family finally gave themselves the freedom to remember their brother, to celebrate a brief life and observe a tragic early death. They shared stories of what the 8, 9, 10-year-old boy was like, and how courageous the little guy had been when facing cancer and his own death. The children in this family had never heard these stories. But the virtues of this boy became part of their larger family story. Part of the testimony.

Advantages and Disadvantages of Using the Family Compound

The family can gather at a destination resort, in a lodge on a lake, or in a college dorm—wherever works. Or they can use a family property, if it fits the gathering's purpose. Patriarchs or matriarchs may assume everyone wants to come home. But the reason many have moved away may be that home does not have a draw for them. A third neutral location can inspire people to focus on the important matters at hand. **Choose the gathering location to align with the values, vision, and mission of the family.**

Sometimes the gathering may be small by design. A client bought a place in Charleston on the water. His large family lives mainly in the Southeast. He has a boat and lake toys. Rather than a big reunion-type psychology, Johnny is intentional with the condo. "Hey, who wants to use the condo?" It's big enough for two families to be there together. At the end of an intense family business meeting, Johnny says, "Mom and I are going down to the condo. Anybody else going?" It's a place that's convenient, an hour away, and that allows for a lot of interaction and community building in an informal, unstructured setting. In his family, that works well. When it's somebody's birthday he'll say, "How many of you want to go down?" Johnny is always intentional, thinking about how a gathering is going to build relationships. This has been good for the family.

On the other hand, Jedd has a place on Lake Michigan. He's got boats, personal water craft, and ski-everything. His expectation is, "By gum, you kids, the four of you, are going to be up here at Thanksgiving. I've spent all this money, and that's what Mom likes." Jedd's intentions are not as pure, leaning into control. Visiting the lake became an obligatory process that was actually destroying family unity until one daughter spoke up. "You know, Dad, we appreciate your generosity and all that you've done. But now we have two boys and there's another set of grandparents involved at Thanksgiving, so we'll probably be there every other year." The Next Gen had to step up and set some boundaries because Dad couldn't hold the place loosely enough.

Celebrate the Journey

Stories from the lives of the founding and other preceding generations never cease to inspire new generations. **If the lessons learned that formed the testimony become embedded in stories-from-the-life-of, these are family treasure.** They give life to testimony.

Your unique family story provides roots and represents a journey through generations. The unique story is wound around the Founder's testimony, that has been formulated in values, vision, and mission. The story started with the Founder, or perhaps with the parents of the Founder. This story should be told often and well, in different ways and settings.

But the story doesn't end there. Next chapters are continually being written and blank pages need to be provided. **A best practice is that the family story should be journey driven, not fact or achievement driven.** You want to capture the anecdotes and the snapshots of the formative reasons why things happened as they did in the family and the business through each generation. You're after accounts of the struggles, not just the triumphs. The failures and detours as well as successes. A journey-driven story like this is easier and more personal for people to tell once the pressure is off to only show success.

Ultimately you want succeeding generations to be able to build a composite of character traits and personalities that give a sure sense of perennial legacy. **Try to get family members to share first-hand account stories to lift the narrative from numbers and objective facts to how experiences helped shape them and the people around them.** There are a variety of ways to capture these stories and you might want to use more than one method or find what works best for your tribe.

Family Communication Platform

An online platform can serve as a family vault for collecting and preserving photographs, stories, documents, and video. You probably have just the right family member to coordinate this. Through KairosWest we offer clients access to a portal powered by WishLife that provides a guide to help you get started. You can share access to the vault with whomever you'd like. As WishLife says, "Letting yourself be known is the most generous and precious gift you can make." WishLife provides story prompts to help elicit good storytelling.

The beauty of a family communication platform is that several family members or different ages can contribute and can access materials. Since the platform is dynamic, it can be updated and expanded continuously.

Priming the Pump: Questions for Family Story Telling

Be intentional about creating opportunities for good family storytelling. Gather as many of the family as possible in one room, all hearing the same stories. Be intentional about it, whether the family event is big or small, because this is a time to build relationships.

It generally takes a facilitator to initiate and move along the telling and capturing of family stories. As a gentleman of the Greatest Generation said to a writer about to begin his legacy book project, "My son told me he doesn't want to just know what I did. He wants to know how I felt about it." Someone may need to guide your family to enable the depth of storytelling that represents what you really want to know. Often repetitive storytelling is a defense mechanism for a family member who is trying to convey an important family value.

Remember that you want to capture the stories of all family members, because the journey continues through them, even the very young ones. One way to get to their stories, their parts of the family journey, is to ask questions. There should be is no right or wrong answers to the questions, so that the answers are personal opinions not open to debate, but potentially reveal interesting insights about the speaker. Questions can be asked by a facilitator or during a meal. Questions can be written inside place cards at a table or projected on a screen. Here are some samples. These are the sorts of questions that you can ask to bring out the "more:"

- What do you wish you knew about an ancestor who has passed away?
- What is something you've started of which you're proud? Where did you get the idea? Who helped you and how? What were your biggest challenges or road blocks?
- Did faith color an important life decision?
- Did you serve in the military? What did you learn from that experience?
- What is a failure you wish you could do over?
- What is a situation in which you've felt afraid or inadequate?
- Share a favorite memory of a family member other than a parent or sibling.
- What are one or two words that you think describe our family?
- Tell about an experience that changed the course of your life.
- If you had the opportunity to pursue another profession, what would it be?
- Tell us a little about your spiritual journey.

Sample Questions for Family Story Telling

What do you wish you knew about an ancestor who has passed away?

What is something you've started of which you are proud?
Where did you get the idea?
Who helped you and how?
What were your biggest challenges or road blocks?

Share a favorite memory of a family member other than a parent or sibling.

What are one or two words that you think describe our family?

Tell about an experience that changed the course of your life.

What is something you're good at?

Whom do you admire and why?

Tracking the Journey

Unfortunately, there is eventually a too lateness to capturing stories from older generations. It's easy to think, "Dad loves to tell stories. We've all heard Dad's stories." It seems like there is plenty of time to capture them in a fixed format. Dad's active. He's talking. But we don't know how long that will last. And no one else knows the whole story like he does. After Dad is no longer sharp and his memory no longer reliable, you might think that family members can still record what they've heard from him…but they don't. Don't put off this process. It's easy to think that this would be a good retirement project. But Dad may just want to play golf when that comes, and the opportunity is lost.

There are many ways to celebrate your family journey by documenting it. We have found utilizing a third party, such as a personal historian to help collect family stories whether it's to an online family vault, on video, collecting photos and creating a slideshow, on audio recordings, or in a published legacy book.

By emphasizing and celebrating the family journey, and the contribution of family members of each generation, you are inspiring and empowering rising generations.

You are imbibing them with the family's values, vision, and mission, which is a best practice of perennial families. **Storytelling can help smooth leadership transition by memorializing the retiring generation and opening a new chapter for the rising leader.** Stories are the tapestries woven of Kairos moments.

Fertilizer

One of our client families uses a simple activity that holds them together well. Each year when they gather they employ a professional photographer to take a photo of the entire group. On the back of the photograph each person has a column in which to write a brief summary of their year: best part, worst part, and a goal for the next year. Everyone gets a copy of both sides of the photograph. Managing this is a great task for someone who usually doesn't have an up-front role. They may be paid to do this job for the family. Use your conative test to see for whom this role would be a good fit.

- Create an on-line family story vault at https://kairos.wishlife.com/
- Contact a personal historian to write a legacy book of your family story. For example, www.Retelling.net

- You can even create a coloring book for the kids from family photographs so that they can color in great-grandpa in his car or a favorite horse or a hot-air balloon ride. Contact Cory Will, Founder of Color Me Book at the website, MyColorMeBook.com.

Our time, stories, lessons learned, values, vision, and mission—our testimony—is the key to multigenerational wealth, not the wills and trusts that dictate the rules and how to comply.

8

The Abundant
Family Garden

EACH PERSON, EACH GENERATION has their strengths and weaknesses. The non-negotiable is that time moves on. We all pass away. When we do, how much of our testimony lives on? I have seen time and time again that THIS is the key to multigenerational wealth. Not the wills and trusts that we set up, but rather our time, stories, lessons learned, values, vision, and mission—our testimony.

If someone spent 100% of their time leading and mentoring their family in Kairos-thinking and did not even have a will or power of attorney, I believe that estate would be more successful, powerful, and vibrant than a family that had the best trust documents with no values, vision, or mission. This is a self-fulfilling prophecy because many families who have great Kairos stories, or a great sense of testimony, values, vision, and mission, also have great estate plans. But the estate plan came from Kairos moments and not the other way around. Kairos can bring us to action and keep us moving forward no matter our credo, skill set, or beliefs. Investing in important relationships always creates a yield. The scale of the yield is what we then try to increase, but it always creates a yield.

That is why we have written this book. It is a collection of best practices from some of the best Kairos families out there, some lessons learned the hard way. We hope that it serves as a seed that can flourish into a great forest of moments for you. Kairos is a pursuit—a sometimes frustrating but valuable one—and not a destination. We believe best practices to be a great medium for growth and vibrancy of a family and enterprise.

Often a guide, or at minimum someone to listen to you as you talk about Kairos things, can be of great value. We have a team that can help you along this journey and discuss best practices. If we could be of help please reach out to us at www.KairosWest.com. Enjoy the journey!

Acknowledgements

Bear with me while I return to this story that involves those people whom I particularly want to thank. It was one of those tough days when you go your hardest and you end up further defeated than when you started. When you gave it your all, and yet today it was not enough.

I was sitting outside our small barn on our colorful hammock swing that we obtained in Guatemala (playing soccer with children from an education support center). I was just sitting, not ready to go inside yet. A bang and desperate cry erupted overhead in the barn roof. Tottenham the barn cat had noticed my presence and yearned for my company. I rescued him from the isolation of the barn and together, Tottenham and I, sat there on the swing and chilled. It was exactly what I needed. Tots was a silent companion to commiserate with after a busy day.

Ellie, my seven-year-old, ran up, joy incarnate. She looked at my white custom dress shirt that was now thoroughly covered in black cat hair and said, "Sometimes it's better to make a memory and go change your shirt afterwards." She didn't say this as a declaration or exoneration but rather a simple statement of wisdom.

This is Kairos to me. I cannot tell you exactly what my dry cleaner charges to clean a dress shirt or how many white dress shirts I have. I can tell you that Tottenham, Ellie, and I all found that time to be fulfilling. Actually, within five minutes I was surrounded by my family and we were having a lovely conversation over a fun fizzy drink my wife had whipped up, the perfect shift to a great evening. My life is blessed by my family who understand and live Kairos daily.

Most of all, I would like to thank these three energetic and dynamic ladies in my family. My wife Stephanie in many ways taught me almost everything I know about Kairos. In my younger years many people gave me the compliment of being "driven." Steph helped me pick my head up and literally smell the roses. I remember on our ten-year anniversary in England we literally walked around and smelled roses for over half an hour (the yellow ones in the back corner of the courtyard were the best). From that day forth I rarely walk by a flower without stopping and smelling.

Adeline, my oldest daughter, stretches me every day. At the age of ten she has already surpassed me in the art of driving to do your very best and going as hard as you can handle, yet stopping to listen to someone like her little sister even though she tends to ramble. Truly listen, with interest and engagement even though it may not benefit her. I hope and pray Adeline grows up to be more like herself and not like me. This skill of caring listening is one I am still working to develop.

Ellie, my youngest daughter, is chock full of Kairos. One of my callings from God is to protect and enable it to come out. These thoughts in a precious young one are often so fragile you worry an errant whisper could blow them a way. My prayer is that God protect her love of her fellow men and women and that I am a good listener in the role he has given me. She was embarrassed to the point of tears when she found out that we knew that she had given my nephew her most prized possession, her Claire's gift card, and all the money she had so he could purchase his fiancé a beautiful engagement ring. That Claire's ring will be more significant with Kairos than the fancy one the jeweler puts together.

I want to thank my brother in Christ and partner in Kairos, Jeff Photiades. It is shocking the parallel daily path God has put us on. Often when I struggle with something I call Jeff, and he is struggling with the exact same thing, and vice versa. He has always been better at being vulnerable and usually calls me first. I love every call.

"Well done is better than well said" is my favorite quote from Benjamin Franklin. My friend Dan Vecchiarelli embodies this statement. His engagement and the love he has for his family and those around him are actually where the inspiration of the Kairos Group came from. Thank you, Dan, for showing me to how to learn via Kairos moments, as you have invested in me many times in this way. May I grow into a Kairos teacher as you are.

When pondering the concept of best practices, the first person who came to mind was Taylor Kirkpatrick. I often marvel how much better a man he is than I. He works harder than most that were born with nothing. He often reminds me of the poem "The True Gentleman" by John Walter Wayland. If you have not read that before you should take a quick break and read it. That is Taylor Kirkpatrick!

Experience is earned. The person on the planet earth that I know with the most experience with families in business transition is Jay Brenneman. While some other gentlemen have focused on winning the "beauty pageant" in the industry of family counseling, Jay constantly returns to the mattresses and gets the important work done. My understanding is this drive is rooted in his deep faith and following of Jesus Christ his Lord and Savior. He has forgotten more best practices in multigenerational wealth than I will ever learn.

I have had a steady stream of wonderful men mentors who literally molded the best parts I have today. Without them I would be very simple and annoyingly selfishly driven. Armen Khadiwala, Dutch Franz, Brian Cunningham, Tim Coan, Dan Vecchiarelli, and John Benson, thank you for all your touches of Kairos in my life.

Finally, a large thank you to my parents. My father has always focused on Kairos to the best of his ability, from garage sale flags to mark a birthday to caroling around the neighborhood. Without my mother, this book would literally not be written. She is the support in so many lives including my own. You are wonderful parents who equipped me in love and continue to teach me to this day. Thank you and love you guys!

About the Authors

Daniel R. Lagerborg

In his career as a tenured, award-winning wealth manager, Daniel R. Lagerborg has been in over 11,000 client meetings and has observed many families, successful and otherwise. He learned that the fabric of success in family wealth is not in efficiency but rather in relationships amongst his clients who sought what he defines as Kairos moments. He works with families to create a safe and sophisticated place in which they can provide for that which is most important to them, especially when faith and family are the most important things.

Taylor Kirkpatrick

Taylor is President & CEO of Babson Farms, a family office overseeing operating businesses in agriculture and insurance, diverse real estate investments, energy interests, and public and private equity investments. He currently chairs a regional family office organization and has presented nationally on topics related to private investments, succession, philanthropy, and educating the rising generation. Prior to Babson Farms, he worked in M&A and financial services. He has extensive strategic planning and leadership experience; he serves on the boards of several private companies and nonprofits and is proud to be a mentor to many in his community.

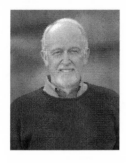

Jay Brenneman

Jay is a Principal in SageQuest Consulting with well over 30 years of experience as a counselor and advisor to family business owners and their families. By integrating a graduate education in psychology at Denver University, an agrarian upbringing, and faith he's guided family business founders and next generation leaders in many industries through the turbulence of business succession. His unique approach to strategic leadership coaching, executive team development, conflict resolution training, and legacy building has helped business owning families preserve both family relationships and the family enterprises.

Made in the USA
Las Vegas, NV
25 June 2021